Celtic Art
in Britain before the Roman Conquest

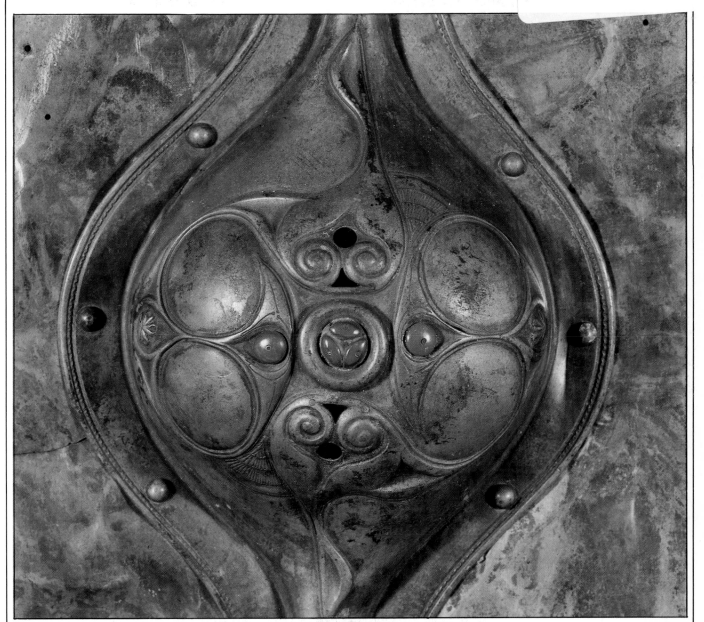

I.M. STEAD

HARVARD UNIVERSITY PRESS
Cambridge, Massachusetts
1985

**THE TRUSTEES OF THE BRITISH MUSEUM
acknowledge with gratitude the
generosity of
THE HENRY MOORE FOUNDATION
for the grant which made possible the
publication of this book**

Front cover Detail from the
red 'enamel' and bronze
roundel at the centre of the
Battersea shield (see
pp. 56 – 7).

Inside front cover The
Brentford 'horn-cap' (see
pp. 18, 65). Height 62mm.

Title page The central part of
the Witham shield, showing
the beads of coral (see p. 54).

This page One of a hoard of
gold alloy torques found at
Ipswich (see also 47).

Back cover Bronze
horse-mask from Stanwick
(see p. 64). Height 101mm.

Inside back cover Detail of
decoration on the Witham
shield (see also title page
and 3).

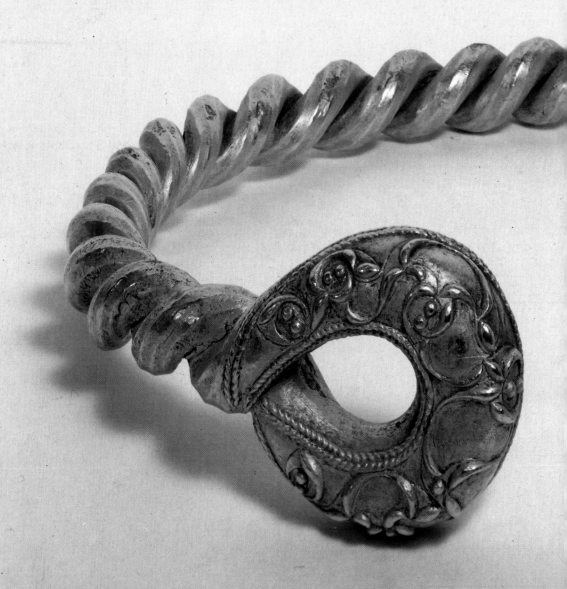

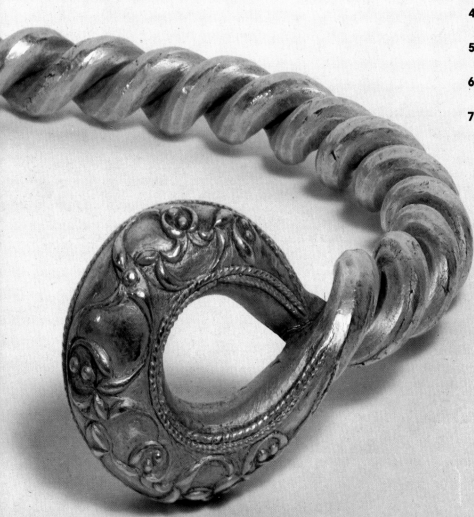

Contents

Introduction

This book is concerned with the British Iron Age, the five hundred years or so before the birth of Christ, when England, Wales and part of Scotland were inhabited by the Celtic-speaking Britons. Their language, British, was spoken but never written, so it is hardly surprising that their written history is brief, comprising a few references in Greek and Latin mainly by writers who knew very little about those remote islands at the edge of the world. But three Latin writers did visit Britain, and the earliest and most important was Julius Caesar, who organised military expeditions here in 55 and 54 BC. Before Caesar history has little to say about Britain, and not a single Briton is known by name. A little can be gleaned from accounts of their relatives, the Gauls, where one of the most important sources is Posidonius (135 – 51 BC), a Greek ethnographer whose lost work was used in the first century BC by Diodorus Siculus, Strabo and even Caesar. But most information about the Britons has to come from the discipline of the prehistorian. By the study of artefacts, excavation, field-work and aerial photography masses of facts can be accumulated about certain aspects of their life; but in the absence of the written word much about the Britons will never be known.

Without chronicles a time-scale has to be constructed, and this is a laborious process bedevilled by uncertainties. Modern techniques are of little help: Carbon-14 dating, for instance, which is vital for the earlier stages of prehistory, is of little use for this period. The date of one very important [1] deposit in a pit at Gussage All Saints (Dorset) is estimated by C 14 to be between 355 and 20 BC, but the chances of the true date falling within these limits is only 68 per cent. The margin of error is huge, and such dates are in any case only rarely associated with significant artefacts. For the immediately pre-Roman period dendrochronology – the counting of tree-rings – is a far more exact technique: it has shown, for instance, that a wooden shield found near the edge of Lake Neuchâtel in Switzerland was shaped from a tree felled in 229 BC. But well-preserved wood survives only in exceptional circumstances, and sequences of tree-rings are only just beginning to extend into the pre-Roman period in Britain. For the material in this book chronology is derived from artefacts – their typology and associations.

The first attempts to construct a chronology for European prehistory were made in the nineteenth century and were based on the materials man used for his basic tools: three Ages were defined, of Stone, Bronze and Iron. The latest, the Iron Age, was subdivided in 1872 into two periods named after important assemblages recently unearthed. The first took its name from a huge cemetery near the salt mines at Hallstatt in Upper Austria, and the second was called La Tène after a site on the shores of Lake Neuchâtel, where an impressive collection of objects had been found when the water-levels of the Swiss lakes were re-aligned. The two names are applied because, in a very general way, those sites produced artefacts typical of their respective periods: they are no more than type-sites, and there is no suggestion that the cultures they represent originated at those sites — still less that those names would have meant anything at all to the peoples thus labelled by archaeologists.

The La Tène period, which is the main concern of this book, was subdivided into Early, Middle and Late as long ago as 1885 on the basis of the typologies of brooches, swords and scabbards, which throughout Celtic Europe developed along roughly

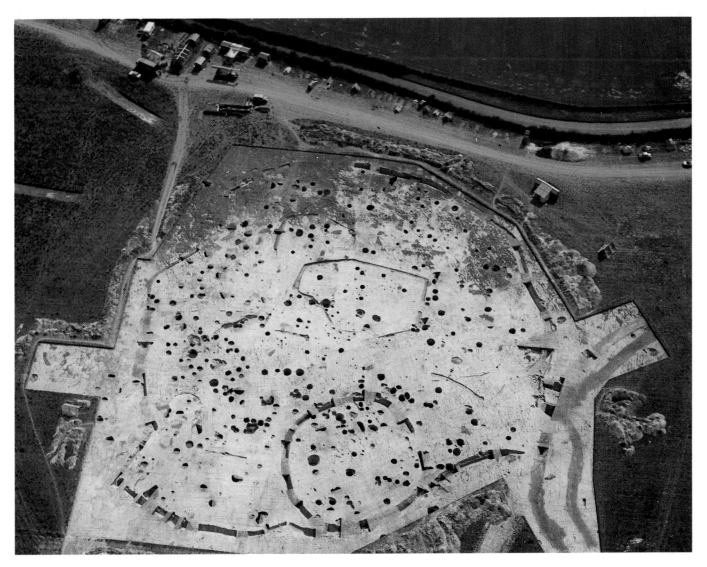

1 Air photograph of the settlement at Gussage All Saints in the course of excavation. Ditches define the settlement (c. 100 × 120m) and some of the buildings; the other prominent features are pits, one of which produced an important collection of metal-working debris.

similar lines. Despite modifications which are valid for certain areas, these subdivisions (or La Tène I, II and III) are still in use. But relative chronology is not an end in itself: it provides a framework to which absolute dates must be attached. Although dendrochronology is already of some help here, it has yet to supersede traditional approaches which rely on dates given by

contacts with the literate civilisations of Greece and Italy. Greek and Latin histories, the occasional discovery of Greek and Italian objects in Celtic graves, and even the odd Celtic object in a classical context enable absolute dates to be applied to Celtic antiquities. The resulting chronology for the La Tène period can be stated only in the most general of terms: La Tène I

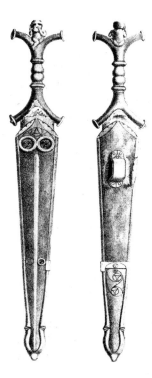

2 Short iron sword with bronze hilt and bronze scabbard, found in the River Witham, but now lost. This illustration was published by Franks in *Horae Ferales* (1863). Full length said to be 15 in. (380mm).

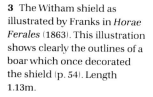

3 The Witham shield as illustrated by Franks in *Horae Ferales* (1863). This illustration shows clearly the outlines of a boar which once decorated the shield (p. 54). Length 1.13m.

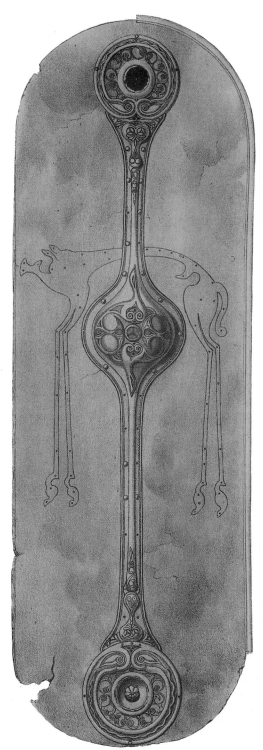

(450 – 250 BC), II (250 – 100 BC) and III (100 BC to the Roman conquest).

Over the centuries Iron Age artefacts must have been found and discarded wherever the ground was tilled or otherwise disturbed. By the eighteenth century, with the industrial and agricultural revolutions, the pace of those disturbances and consequent discoveries increased and coincided with a growing interest in history and antiquities. One of the earliest recorded Iron Age artefacts in Britain is a Celtic bronze carnyx (trumpet) – still the most complete example known – found when the River Witham in Lincolnshire was being dredged in 1768. It was acquired by Sir Joseph Banks, a local worthy and a scholar with an international reputation, who allowed a zealous scientist to destroy it in order to determine its composition. Other antiquities dredged from the Witham have also been lost, including a remarkable short sword in a bronze scabbard: the hilt **2** is of bronze and its pommel was represented (perhaps misrepresented) as a kind of Lincoln imp. In the eighteenth century some antiquities found their way into cabinets of curiosities, but in the nineteenth century collectors took to the field: in 1815 the Rev. E. W. Stillingfleet 'joined a party, which was formed for the purpose of opening a group of barrows' at Arras (North Humberside) and came across Iron Age skeletons with grave-goods as rich as any yet found in Britain. By the middle of the century a considerable number of Iron Age antiquities were known, mainly chance finds and including some remarkable pieces dredged from the Thames and the Witham. Many were published by A. W. **3** Franks in an outstanding contribution to *Horae Ferales* (1863): Franks saw the British **4** antiquities in a European context, and was ahead of his Continental colleagues in

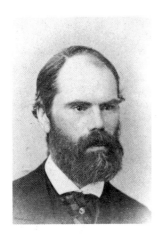

recognising them as Celtic. Since then the pace of archaeological excavation has gradually increased, producing a steady stream of antiquities for the museums, but despite the efforts of archaeologists – and metal-detectors – the finest pieces of Celtic art are still found by chance.

For every metal object that was buried, either deliberately or by chance, there must have been many more that were used until they were broken, worn or obsolete and then recycled. The surviving sample is minute. Caesar mentioned 4,000 chariots retained by the British king Cassivellaunus, and each of those chariots would have been drawn by two horses, each with a horse-bit and with shared harness using five terrets (rein-rings). Of those 8,000 horse-bits and 20,000 terrets is there a single one in our museums today? Prob-

ably not. Even the small sample now available for study may be distorted, because objects that were deliberately buried may well have been specially selected and need not be typical of the objects of the day. With pottery the problems are not so marked: pots are fragile when in use, are readily broken and only a tiny percentage are recycled, but once they are buried either complete or in sherds they are well-nigh indestructible. As well as metal and pottery a vast range of organic materials such as wood, skin and fabrics was much used by the Celts, as by all primitive peoples. These materials gradually deteriorate in use and only a small percentage would be buried; unless they were deposited in an exceptional environment their deterioration would then be accelerated. In our climate only waterlogged conditions will preserve organic materials, and the sample available for study is negligible.

Most Celtic art takes the form of abstract decoration on functional objects, which would have appealed to the Celt because of its meaning or usefulness but which is also in tune with current taste. Sensitive and appreciative modern writers have made valiant efforts to interpret its meaning, but the imagination of modern man is an unreliable guide to the aims, beliefs and feelings of his primitive forebears. Only the Celtic artist and his patrons could explain Celtic art, and as they never set pen to paper their knowledge died with them. This book attempts to approach the subject on fairly solid ground, starting with techniques of metalwork (because most surviving examples are made of metal) then following the development of certain patterns, and finally giving examples of decorated artefacts used by the Britons in various walks of life.

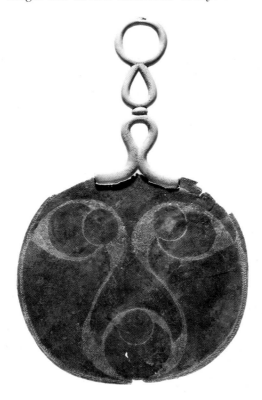

5 Bronze mirror, decorated on the back, from Aston (Herts.). The mirror-plate was found by a farmer in 1979; the handle was discovered in a subsequent archaeological excavation. Diameter 194mm.

1 Metalworking techniques

Bronze had already been worked in Britain for over a millennium before the Iron Age began, but it was still of prime importance – particularly for decorative work. Most soils are gentler to bronze than to iron, and apart from a usually greenish patina much of it differs little from the day when it was lost or discarded. Bronze is an alloy of copper and tin, and judging from analyses it was carefully mixed to obtain a precise balance between the two. Copper was mined in the south-west of England, in Wales, Scotland and Ireland, and Cornish tin was well known in the ancient world and attracted explorers from as far afield as Greece. But foreign ores were also used in Britain, for Caesar records that bronze was imported and analyses have shown that this practice went back into the Bronze Age. Sheet bronze was made by casting an ingot and beating it into a thin sheet; then it could be cut by shears and decorated in various ways. Some of the more ambitious products, such as the famous shield bosses, were decorated by repoussé – raising the design by hammering from the underside, with the object presumably resting on a bed of resilient pitch. Relatively small pieces were mass-produced by using a 'former' into which a master design had been cut: both iron and bronze formers are known but wood could also have been used. The sheet bronze to be decorated would then be placed over the former and beaten into the recessed shapes to create a number of identical patterns. Some of the decoration on the Aylesford bucket was made in this way: of the three designs on its upper band two occur four times and one twice – each time the impressions are identical. In at least one place, at the side of the 'pantomime horses', there is an im-

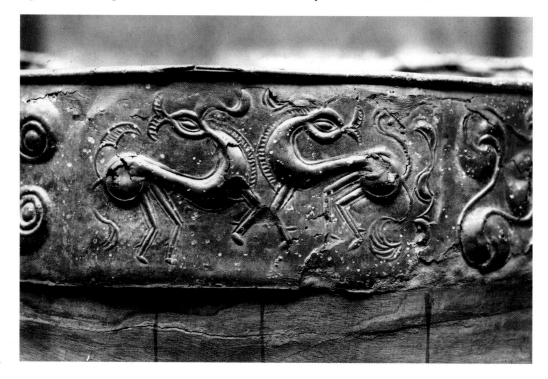

6 A detail of the decoration on the Aylesford bucket (see 53). The two fantastic animals have been shaped in a former, and there is an identical impression on the opposite side of the bucket. The vertical edges of the former can be distinguished, especially on the right.

6

7 Detail of a silicone rubber mould of decoration on the back of the Great Chesterford (Essex) mirror. Engraved with a common graver and a fine round-nosed graver (possibly the same tool, the edge of which was changed by resharpening); 'guide lines' are lightly scratched by a scriber.

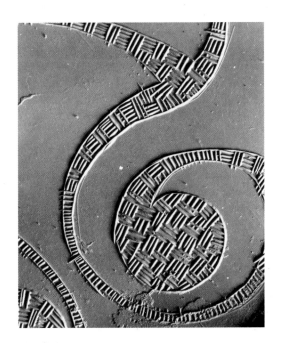

pression of a vertical line which may well have been made by the edge of a former.

Surface decoration was sometimes inscribed or scratched using a fine-pointed scriber to produce a sharp line. This tool was used alone in some designs, but in others it was employed for the preliminary mapping out. More pronounced lines were engraved with a graver, which was drawn over the surface and held in the fingers rather as one would hold a pencil; a somewhat similar effect was produced by chasing which involved a tracer being hammered forward across the metal. If the marks are well preserved it should be possible to identify the tools that made them and in some instances it has been possible to follow the development of the tool in the course of the work — such as the stages at which its edge was chipped and subsequently resharpened. Unfortunately the fine tools themselves are difficult to identify. More substantial tools are easier

to recognise and a collection from a grave at Whitcombe (Dorset) comprised an iron hammer-head and file as well as a chalk disc which could have served as the fly-wheel for a pump-drill. Iron files can sometimes be identified with the aid of radiography, and examples from Fiskerton (Lincs.) and Gussage All Saints (Dorset) had specks of bronze in the grooves showing that they had been used by bronze-workers.

Sometimes the bronze-smith tried out the effects of a tool on part of an object that would be hidden from view. On the Birdlip mirror, for instance, there are practice tool-marks in the area subsequently covered by the bronze handle. Similarly a design had been roughly worked on the inner face of a scabbard-plate found in the River Bann in Northern Ireland. Bone would have been an ideal medium on which to sketch designs intended for bronze, and a collection of bone flakes with compass-drawn ornament from Lough Crew (Co. Meath) seems to have been used in this way. Their context is curious, because they were found in a tomb which would then have been some 3,000 years old. Amongst the Lough Crew finds was what may well have been a pair of compasses (now lost) and it seems reasonable to interpret the collection as workshop debris. Compasses were undoubtedly used by some Celtic artists and very complex designs were constructed. Detailed study of the decoration on the back of the Holcombe mirror has shown that it could have been formed entirely from compass arcs, and some grooves on its surface can only have been made by heavy scratching with compasses. Designs could have been laid out directly on the bronze by first coating it with a thin layer of wax and using something like a transparent slice of horn below the centre-point to ensure that it did not mark the metal surface.

Another way of producing decorative bronze-work was by lost-wax casting. The object was first modelled in wax – and sometimes elaborately decorated at this stage – then encased in clay, heated to melt and remove the wax, and fired to harden the clay. Bronze of a slightly different alloy from sheet bronze – lead was added to increase the fluidity – poured into this fired clay mould would take on the exact form of the modelled wax. The fired clay would have to be broken open – the mould could never be used again – before the bronze object was finished by filing, polishing and perhaps by the addition of more detail using the tools already described for decorating sheet bronze. This method of production must have created a huge quantity of broken moulds, but very few have been recognised. The best collection was discovered in pit 209 on the settlement at Gussage All Saints where more than 7,000 fragments of moulds had been discarded. The Gussage bronze-smith, who had been making harness and chariot fittings, had had a workshop on the site but nothing of it survived: it is known simply because some of the debris was swept up and dumped in a pit. Amongst the rubbish were some of the tools used for modelling the wax. Ironically these fragile bone implements are still in perfect condition, whereas the hard steel tools used by the same craftsman have been reduced to virtually unrecognisable lengths of corrosion products.

Cast bronze was used to make some complete objects, but it was also a component of more complex objects. Sword scabbards were sometimes made of bronze: two scabbard-plates would be cut from the sheet, one wrapped round the edges of the other, and their lower parts secured by a sheet bronze chape. But the very end of the chape was usually cast-on to the frame. The bronze-smith must have worked in close co-operation with the blacksmith – sometimes perhaps the same craftsman carried out both trades in the same workshop. Pit 209 at Gussage All Saints included scale produced by forging iron as well as moulds for casting bronze. Bronze was cast-on to iron to make vehicle fittings and harness, and sometimes iron was covered with bronze, either dipped in molten bronze or, as with the rings of many horse-bits, encased in sheet bronze.

Iron was first worked in Britain in the seventh century BC. More widespread and plentiful, and therefore cheaper, iron ores

8

9

9

9 *Right* The end of a bronze scabbard from Bugthorpe (N. Humberside). The sheet bronze front-plate, decorated with an engraver or tracer, is attached to an iron back-plate by the binding strips of a chape, also cut from sheet bronze. The chape-end has been cast-on to the binding strips and its decoration is part of the lost-wax casting. Width of chape-end 43mm.

8 *Below* Bone modelling tools, fired clay moulds (for a link of a horse-bit, *above*, and the head of a linch-pin, *below*) and the corroded remains of iron or steel tools. From pit 209 at Gussage All Saints. Length of bone tool (left) 82mm.

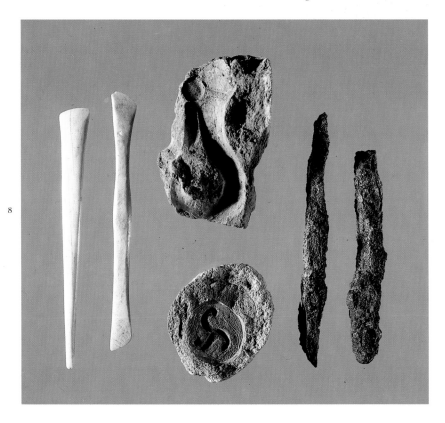

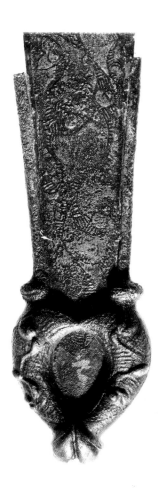

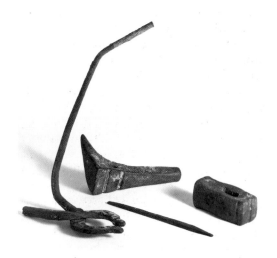

were usually obtained from shallow open-cast workings in close proximity to the woodland needed to provide charcoal for smelting. One of the earliest iron-producing sites in Britain might well have been at Brooklands, near Weybridge (Surrey), where a well-known deposit of iron ore was still being worked in the nineteenth century. The date of the Iron Age workings at Brooklands is difficult to establish because the only associated artefacts – mainly coarse pottery – are imprecisely dated, but it is tempting to link them with an imported Hallstatt C bronze bucket found only 100m away. Remains of iron-smelting furnaces excavated at Brooklands are no more than a simple bowl which would have been surmounted by a fired clay shaft: there was no provision for tapping the slag which would have collected in the bottom, so that the furnace had to be dismantled to remove both bloom and slag. Iron could not be worked in the same way as bronze; for instance, it does not melt at the temperatures achieved in the Iron Age. Instead, the smelted bloom was forged, which means that the iron was repeatedly brought to a red heat and hammered to produce the finished object. Both smelting and forging were carried out at Brooklands.

The Iron Age blacksmith seems to have had most of the skills and most of the tools used by village blacksmiths until recent times. His hallmark is the long-handled tongs needed to hold the red-hot iron at a comfortable distance. A small hoard of ironwork from Waltham Abbey (Essex) included the tools of a blacksmith; those that could be broken had been deliberately smashed, presumably as part of a ritual, before the hoard was deposited in the River Lea. As well as five pairs of tongs, the blacksmith's tools included three small

10 *Right, above* Some of the blacksmiths' tools from the Waltham Abbey hoard: tongs, anvil, head of a sledge-hammer and file. The anvil and the head of the sledge-hammer have been grooved so that they could be used as swages. The file is 232mm long.

11 *Right, below* Head of an iron fire-dog found at Baldock; the complete fire-dog is 700mm high.

10

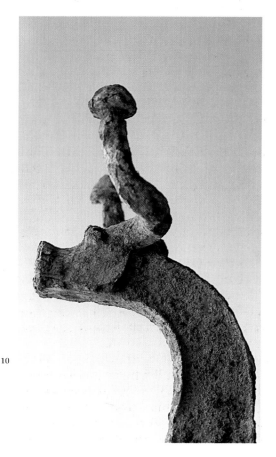

anvils, the head of a sledge-hammer, a file and a poker, in a collection dating from the first century BC or AD. Two of the anvils are particularly interesting: they could be reversed for use as mandrels (over which bars and rods could be bent) and were also grooved for rounding metal rods. The rods would be shaped between an upper and a lower groove, or swage: in the Waltham Abbey collection the anvils served as the lower swages and the head of the sledge-hammer had been grooved to double as an upper swage. Multi-purpose tools like these suggest that the blacksmith was itinerant because he seems to have been anxious to keep the number of heavy tools to a minimum. Ancient tools are by no means common because they would have been highly prized and passed from one generation to another, and when worn out they would have been recycled. Unassociated iron tools are difficult to date because the same forms remain in use for centuries, so most blacksmiths' tools of the Iron Age are known only from deliberate deposits in hoards or graves. The Iron Age blacksmith also had hammers, set-hammers, hot-chisels, and slices — a long poker-like tool with a spatulate end used for controlling the hot fuel.

One of the finest products of the Iron Age blacksmith is the fire-dog, and the head from one found at Baldock (Herts.) is an especially impressive piece of work. The tall upright has been bent outwards at the top to form the basis of the head, from which the snout has been forged, the nostrils punched and the mouth and prominent jaw-line chiselled. The horns would have been forged separately, welded on top of the head, and their ends shaped into protruding eyes. Iron could also be engraved or chased, provided the graver or tracer was hard enough, but surface corrosion has left us few good examples.

Of other metals silver, listed by Strabo as a British import, was rarely used by the Celts either in Britain or on the Continent, but the use of gold was widespread. Always valuable, gold objects suffered especially from recycling and many a work of art must have been consigned to the crucible to produce Britain's gold coinage. Alone among the metals, gold does not corrode and comes out of the ground as bright as when it was last seen in the Iron Age. Although they would have worked it in the same way as bronze, the Britons seem never to have used gold for brooches, and only very rarely for bracelets, but gold torques (neck-rings) feature prominently amongst British antiquities. They are particularly well represented in East Anglia where many of them are more correctly classified as electrum, an alloy of gold and silver that occurs naturally. In the first century AD bronze and silver objects were occasionally gilded, but this seems to be due to Roman influence and pre-Roman gilding is unknown in Britain.

Metalwork, especially bronze, was occasionally enhanced by the addition of coloured ornaments. Precious coral from the Mediterranean was applied in the form of beads or strips to a variety of objects, often attached by bronze pins or rivets. Some brooches from the Yorkshire graves have huge amounts of coral, the colour of which has been reduced from pink to white as a result of centuries in the earth. The Witham shield has beads of coral which still *title page* retain their original, very deep, colour. On the Continent coral is rarely used after La Tène I, but in Britain it continued into La Tène III: indeed, coral in the Polden Hill hoard shows that it was still employed at the time of the Roman conquest. Shell, amber and stone ornaments are also

12 The central panel of the Battersea shield (see 77,78) with red 'enamel' decoration. Diameter 290mm.

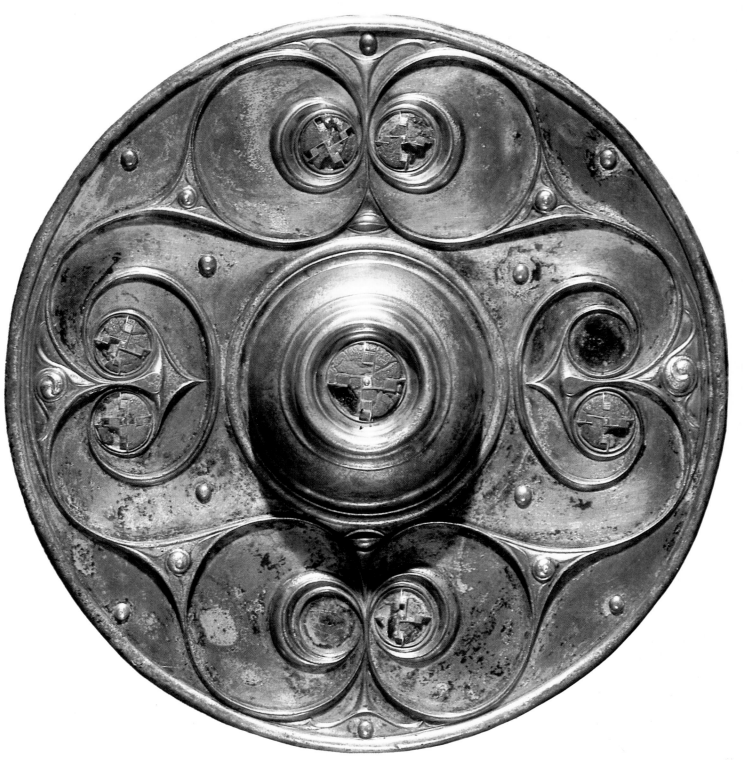

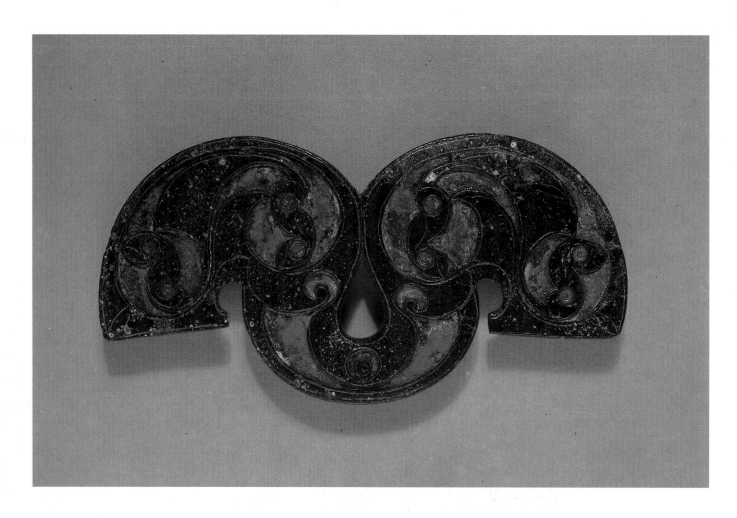

13 Bronze harness-fitting decorated with red champlevé enamel, from the Polden Hill hoard. Length 151mm.

known, but the most common alternative to coral was red glass or 'enamel'. The glass usually has an opaque 'sealing-wax red' colour which is given by crystals of cuprous oxide. It was used in small lumps which could be softened by heating and then shaped into small pellets to be attached by bronze pins; secured onto roughly keyed surfaces; or held by cut-out bronze frames. By the first century AD champlevé enamel was made in some quantity: with this technique a slightly sunken field is prepared either in the original casting or by subsequent cutting, and the enamel is applied as a powder and fused in an oven. The effect is to produce a flat field of enamel whose surface is flush with that of the surrounding metal. Britain was famous for its enamel-work, as Philostratus recorded early in the third century AD: 'they say that the barbarians who live in the Ocean pour [these] colours on to heated bronze and that they adhere, and grow hard as stone, keeping the designs that are made in them'.

2 Art styles

Insular Celtic (or La Tène) art must be studied in a European context, for in the early stages Britain is an outlying province of the Continental tradition. But from the middle of the third century BC British art receives a new impetus, takes its own original direction, and its masterpieces outclass the products of Continental workshops. La Tène art was first classified by Paul Jacobsthal, a distinguished classical archaeologist who left Nazi Germany in the 1930s and settled in England. He had made a detailed study of Continental work, published in a fully illustrated monograph in 1944, but he never completed his study of the British material. On the Continent he recognised three styles: an 'Early Style' strongly influenced by Greek art but with some Oriental and native traits; followed by a more mature 'Waldalgesheim Style', named after a rich grave in the Rhineland; and then two contemporary sub-styles – the 'Sword Style' (though decorating scabbards and not swords) and the 'Plastic Style'. His study ended within La Tène II and did not extend to the Roman conquest.

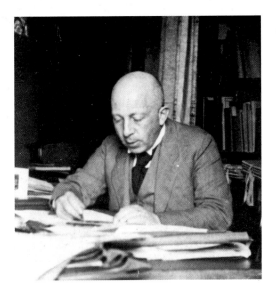

14 Paul Ferdinand Jacobsthal (1880 - 1957), Professor of Classical Archaeology at Marburg University 1912 - 35.

Jacobsthal's classification is still fundamental, although subsequent scholars have indicated its imperfections and suggested improvements. For the 'Early Style' more material is now known from Eastern Europe, and the geometric native element is more pronounced; the 'Waldalgesheim Style' is seen to owe more to further Greek (Graeco-Italian) influences and less to a Waldalgesheim Master; and a 'Swiss Sword Style' has been distinguished from the 'Hungarian Sword Style'.

Jacobsthal's views on British La Tène art are known from his occasional published notes and from the writings of J. M. de Navarro, who had access to at least one of Jacobsthal's unpublished papers. His classification of the earlier British material into numbered styles has been allowed to lapse in recent years, but is here revived and extended because some kind of framework is needed to describe the development of La Tène art and to relate it to other aspects of Celtic culture. Any scheme of classification must generalise and simplify, and this one is no exception: it emphasises some of the major trends but falls well short of encompassing every aspect of Celtic art in Britain. A classification related to the Continental framework but at the same time distinct from it is ideal because even in the early stages the British material seems to have been home-produced, and in the second and first centuries BC it is only remotely linked to Continental developments. The numbered styles have the merit of clarity, the validity of the sequence has been confirmed particularly by the study of British sword scabbards and no alternative classification has ever been proposed.

Style I, which Jacobsthal equated with the 'Early Style', is represented by both native Hallstatt elements and designs ultimately derived from Greek art. The Hall-

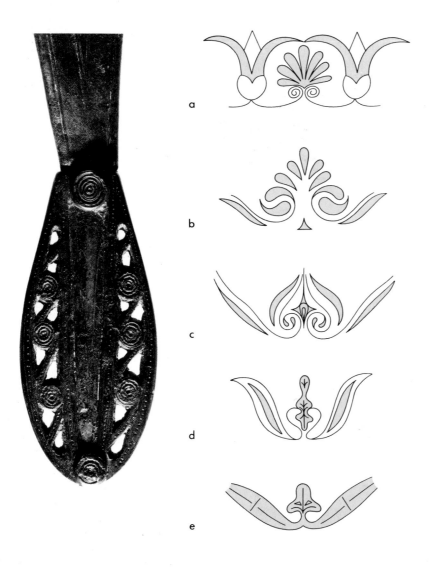

15 Bronze chape on a sheath from Wandsworth, a lost-wax casting featuring concentric circles. Length of chape 66mm.

16 The palmette. Celtic artists borrowed an Etruscan decorative motif, a palmette and lotus flowers, and created their own versions of the palmette, often flanked by lotus petals and arranged in a frieze: a) an Etruscan palmette and lotus flowers; b) a Celtic palmette and lotus petals on an imported Etruscan flagon now in the museum at Besançon; c – e: similar Celtic motifs on c) a bronze disc from Ecury-sur-Coole (Marne); d) a pottery jar from St Pol-de-Léon (Finistère); and e) the flange of a bronze lid from Cerrig-y-Drudion (see 17).

statt designs are extremely simple, sometimes found in the borders of dagger-sheaths and sword scabbards, and include 15 strings of cross-hatched triangles, lozenges and compass-drawn arcs and dots. Such decoration is engraved or chased on bronze or iron pieces dating from the fourth century and the end of the fifth century BC. The most complex of the geometric designs is no more than a series of circles linked by diagonal lines. The more elaborate Style I motifs are based on a Greek design – a floral frieze of palmettes 16 flanked by lotus flowers. This device had a fascination particularly for the Celts in eastern France, who engraved elaborate variations of it on helmets, harness and even on an imported Etruscan flagon – objects which have survived because they were deliberately buried, in graves. In Brittany similar motifs were used on pots. Work in this style may have been widespread in Britain, but only a little early metalwork survives because graves of the period are rare and this form of ornament was never used on British pottery. One of the few burials with metal grave-goods, found in a stone cist at Cerrig-y-Drudion (Clwyd), had been robbed and excavation in 1924 revealed only broken fragments of bronze. However, some of the fragments were from the decorated flange of a lid, possibly two lids, and sufficient survived to piece together half of one design, which features palmettes and 'lotus petals' (16e, 17). There is another version of the same design on a bronze scabbard- or sheath- 18 plate from a collection formed by 'Philosopher' Smith of Wisbech (Cambs.) and presumed to be of local origin.

The principal motif of the 'Waldalgesheim Style' (the British Style II) is influenced by the wave tendril in Greek art 19 and takes the form of a string of triangular

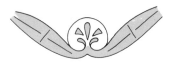

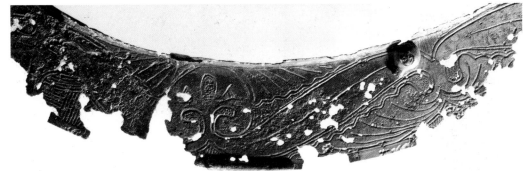

17 Part of the decoration on the flange of a bronze lid from Cerrig-y-Drudion (see also 16e): a version of the palmette flanked by lotus petals (Style I). Width of flange 28mm.

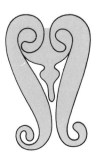

18 Upper part of a bronze sheath-plate from Wisbech with a palmette (cf. 16d and e) flanked by lotus petals or lyres (Style I). Hatched triangles down the sides are in the Hallstatt tradition. Width 48mm.

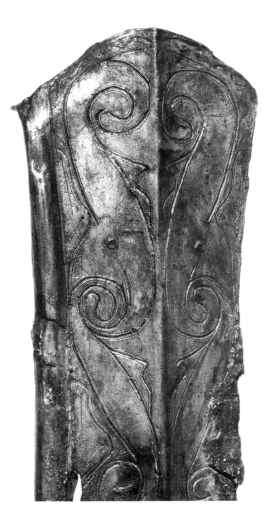

shapes each linked at two corners and with a tendril sprouting from the third. Simple friezes of this type decorate elongated fields, especially on brooches and sword scabbards. There are typical examples in northern Italy, where the Celts came into close contact with classical influences after their invasion early in the fourth century BC, but others are found throughout Celtic lands from Litér in Hungary to Standlake in England. The Standlake scabbard, found in the River Thames, must have been made of wood or leather, but all that survive are two decorative bronze panels. The panel at the foot of the scabbard, within the chape, has 19d a typical Style II tendril, whilst the one at the top has a repoussé pelta-like motif framed by a similar tendril. Both panels have hatched backgrounds, a feature much more common on British than on Continental work. The Standlake scabbard, which has a typical La Tène I chape-end and houses a La Tène I sword, dates from the end of the fourth century or the start of the third century BC. A similar tendril frieze, crudely executed in pointillé, rings the antler handle of an iron rasp found 19e recently at Fiskerton (Lincs.), and there is another example on a heavy cast bronze bracelet from a grave at Newham Croft (Cambs.), where the ornament is in a band

19 *Right* The wave tendril ('Waldalgesheim Style', Style II). Based on a Greek motif, this design is found throughout Celtic Europe; examples are on a) a helmet from Amfreville (France); b) a scabbard from Moscano di Fabriano (Italy); c) a scabbard from Litér (Hungary); and two English pieces: d) a scabbard from Standlake and e) an antler handle from Fiskerton.

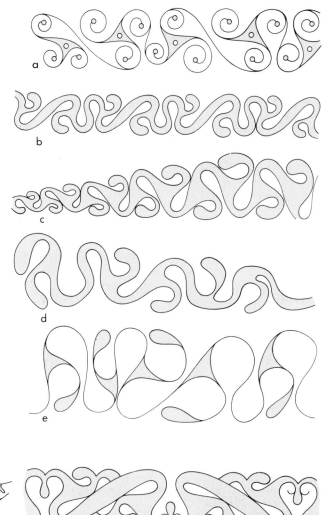

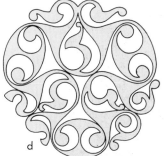

20 Palmettes and tendrils ('Early Style' 'Waldalgesheim Style', Style I/II): a) a helmet from Canosa (Italy); b) a scabbard from Filottrano (Italy); c) a torque from Waldalgesheim (Germany); and d) a 'horn cap' from Brentford (England) – see also inside front cover.

wrapped at an angle round the body of the bracelet. Such angled banded ornament can be matched on the Continent, especially on sword scabbards. The Newnham Croft bracelet is very worn, but some hatching survives and there are hints that the entire background was so treated.

In certain works the 'Waldalgesheim Style' can be clearly distinguished, but in others – and especially in the tradition of the floral motifs – Style II flows from Style I without any sharp break. Triangles and tendrils rise from the sides of palmettes in the engraved 'Early Style' works of eastern France, on the Canosa helmet and Filottrano scabbard from Italy, and on the torque from the Waldalgesheim grave itself. In Britain there is a good example in the design of three linked palmettes on the cast bronze 'horn-cap' from Brentford. This 'horn-cap' is a distinctively British artefact *insi* not found on the Continent. Indeed, *fror* although the British Style II is derived from the Continental 'Waldalgesheim Style' all the objects decorated in it have insular traits and there is no reason to doubt that all were made in Britain.

There is very little in Britain that can be classified as Style III, although the influence of both 'Plastic' and 'Sword' sub-styles is important in the genesis of Style IV. Jacobsthal saw minor elements of his 'Plastic Style' – high relief 'snail-shell coils' – on British brooches from Newnham Croft (the same grave-group as the bracelet) and from Danes Graves, Driffield (N. Humberside), and this tradition may well have influenced masterpieces such as the Wandsworth mask boss. The other sub-division of Style III, the 'Sword Style', may be represented by two British scabbards with dragon-pair ornament (22). This device is found in a panel towards the top of each scabbard and comprises a pair of confronted beasts,

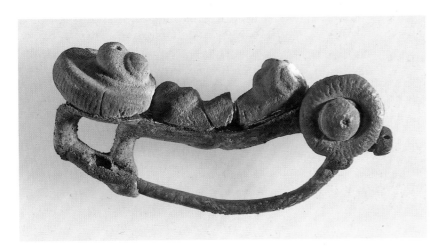

21 A bronze brooch with red-coloured sandstone ornament, from Danes Graves. The 'snail-shell coils' on the foot and bow have been classified as Style III ornament. Length 65mm.

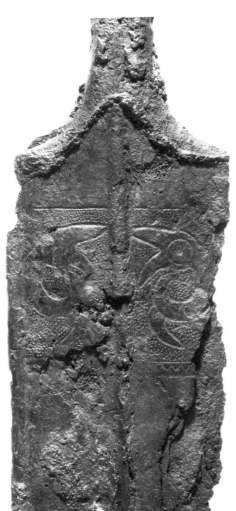

22 Upper part of an iron scabbard with dragon-pair ornament, from Hammersmith. Width of scabbard 51mm.

sometimes interpreted as griffins but now universally classified as dragons. The significance of the design is unknown, of course, but it is difficult to believe that it was intended merely as decoration. In the third century BC, dragon-pairs appear on scabbards across Celtic Europe as far east as Romania and there are some quite remarkable similarities between examples from West and East. Although contemporary with both the 'Swiss' and 'Hungarian Sword' styles, they transcend regional boundaries and have been described as 'an inter-Celtic currency'. Despite their Oriental appearance the earliest dragon-pairs seem to occur in Western Europe, where they may well have originated in the lyre or confronted S-motif: some dragons are little more than an 's' with an eye and an ear. The two English scabbards, both of La Tène I form and made of iron, were found in the River Thames in the middle of last century and are particularly important as unambiguous evidence for close Continental links early in the third century BC.

Style IV was defined by de Navarro in a popular work, but it was never analysed in detail and its unity was not accepted by Jacobsthal, who objected to de Navarro's use of the term. Nevertheless, a number of features can be distinguished, particularly in line ornament, which seem a reasonable basis for defining a style. Some of the designs are based on the Waldalgesheim tendril, but with less regular convolutions, more varied shapes within the stem and tightly coiled spiral terminals. An example was found recently at Fovant (Wilts.) on an iron scabbard which still held its sword. In a panel at the top of the scabbard is a confronted motif surely derived from a dragon-pair, but this graceful design is far removed from the mainly limited repertoire of Continental dragons. The decora-

23

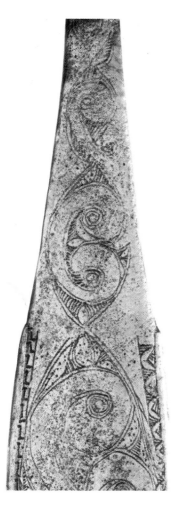

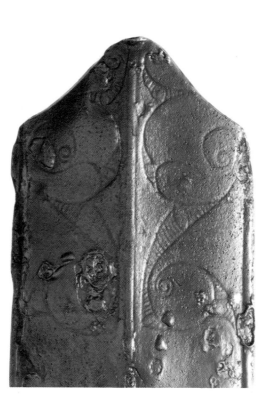

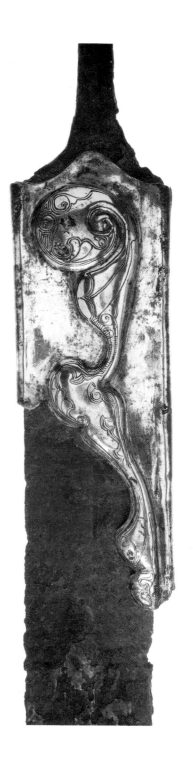

23 Style IV decoration on a bronze scabbard-plate from the River Bann (*left*) and on an iron scabbard-plate from Fovant (*right*). The tightly coiled spirals are typical, and the hatching on the Fovant piece can be matched exactly on the Bann scabbard. The Fovant scabbard is 45mm wide.

tion compares closely with parts of the design on a bronze scabbard-plate from the River Bann, whose entire length and width is covered with an engraved free-hand design. On other pieces, the tendril occasionally curves back and crosses itself, recalling designs of the 'Hungarian Sword Style'.

Another important Style IV motif is the half-palmette, found already on works of the Continental 'Early Style'. It features prominently on the Witham shield, in both repoussé and engraving, and also on the

25 *Right* Style IV motifs. Comparable versions of a tendril crossing itself like a figure-of-eight: a) on the Witham shield; b) on the Wandsworth round boss. The half-palmette: the derivation of c (an example from the cheek-piece of a helmet, probably from Italy) can be seen by reference to 16a; d (on the Witham shield, cf. inside back cover) and e (on the Witham scabbard, cf. 24) are more devolved versions.

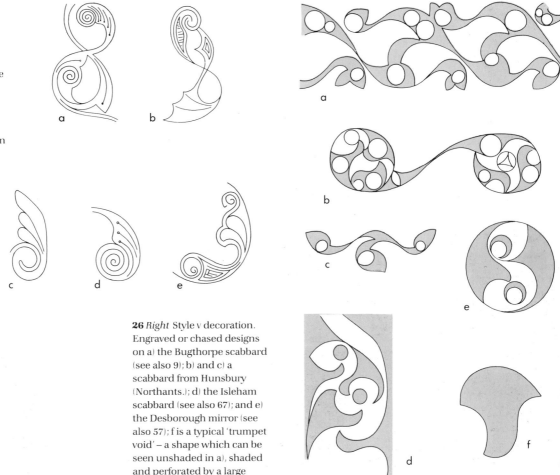

26 *Right* Style V decoration. Engraved or chased designs on a) the Bugthorpe scabbard (see also 9); b) and c) a scabbard from Hunsbury (Northants.); d) the Isleham scabbard (see also 67); and e) the Desborough mirror (see also 57); f is a typical 'trumpet void' – a shape which can be seen unshaded in a), shaded and perforated by a large circle and also unshaded in b), and shaded in d) and e).

24 *Left* Bronze ornament on a scabbard from the River Witham. Width 48mm.

scabbard from that same river. The Witham scabbard seems likely to have been made of wood or leather which has now perished, but the magnificent bronze panel which decorated its mouth is still corroded onto the blade. Beautifully preserved in bright shining bronze, the panel is shaped in repoussé with an outline which crosses the sword diagonally like some of the Hungarian Sword Style designs. The overall shape of this panel may itself be a distorted

half-palmette, and that motif certainly inspired some of the engraving that adorns it.

Style IV, which ends in the second century BC, was the last of the numbered styles defined by de Navarro, but the sequence is here continued with a Style V, which takes the development of British Celtic art through the following century. This is the art style studied especially by Sir Cyril Fox. He did not call it Style V; indeed, he gave it no overall title, although one aspect of it he

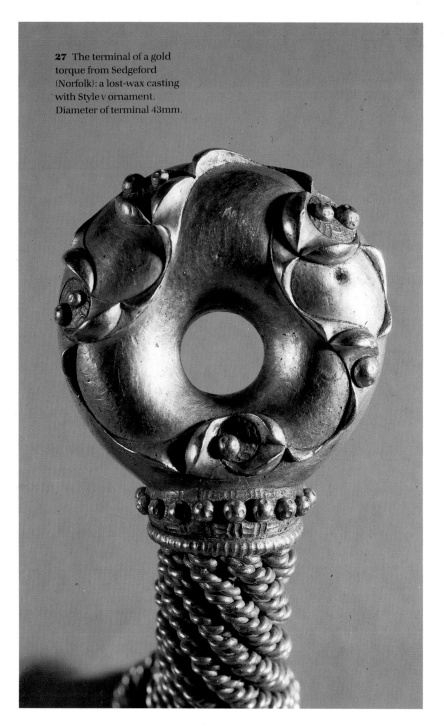

27 The terminal of a gold torque from Sedgeford (Norfolk): a lost-wax casting with Style V ornament. Diameter of terminal 43mm.

called the 'mirror-style'. His interest was aroused by the discovery in 1943 of a huge collection of metalwork at Llyn Cerrig Bach (Anglesey), acquired when he was the Director of the National Museum of Wales. The collection included two magnificent decorated bronzes – a plaque and a shield-boss – the art styles of which were clearly related. In a series of publications Fox analysed the designs and traced the principal motifs in other works across Britain. He was keen to identify regional art styles (schools) and, by tracing the evolution and devolution of designs, he attempted to organise the material in a tight chronological order to which he applied tentative absolute dates.

Style V includes tendril designs in elongated fields, as well as fragments of tendrils in minor panels and more ambitious designs in circular or rectangular frames. Shapes are more curvilinear than in Style IV, fillings are confined to hatching (compare 57 with 64), and often the hatching is interrupted by a circle. Instead of being used only for the design, hatching is sometimes employed as background instead. Tendrils terminate not in a spiral, but in a distinctive 'trumpet' shape which, with an adjoining circle, gives the impression of a bird-head with huge eye and beak – sometimes an open beak. The voids associated with these designs can be as distinctive as the pattern itself, and Fox drew attention to one particular shape – a 'trumpet' void composed of one compound curve (concave/convex) and two simple curves (one concave and the other convex). This shape, sometimes a positive rather than a negative element, can be seen in many Style V designs.

Engraving and chasing were not the only means of producing Style V patterns. Repoussé was popular, and the plaque from

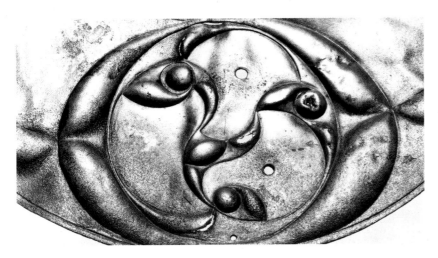

28 Style v decoration in repoussé on a bronze plaque from Llyn Cerrig Bach. Note the three prominent 'trumpet voids' (as 26f) defined by the repoussé shapes. Height 80mm.

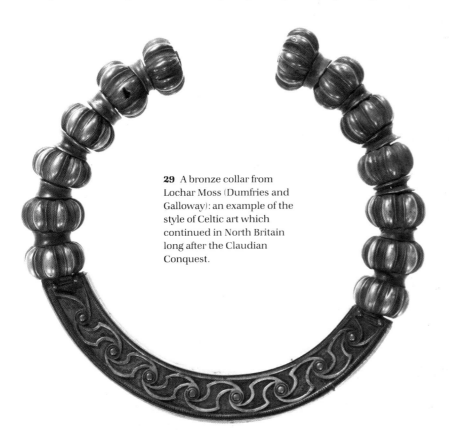

29 A bronze collar from Lochar Moss (Dumfries and Galloway): an example of the style of Celtic art which continued in North Britain long after the Claudian Conquest.

Llyn Cerrig Bach provides a good example, with a design in a small circular panel and the repoussé executed in two planes. The motif is basically a triskele or triquetra — a three-limbed device used throughout the history of Celtic art and perhaps best-known on the Isle of Man coat of arms. On the plaque the triskele is built from repoussé lobes; each limb ends in a 'trumpet' and a boss and the whole is framed by lobes. On other pieces Style v ornament is achieved by lost-wax casting, which can produce relief lobes and hatched backgrounds. Sometimes a single piece has ornament in different techniques, presumably made in the same workshop: the Bugthorpe (N. Humberside) scabbard has engraved ornament on the front-plate and a decorated cast chape-end, whereas a Little Wittenham (Oxon.) scabbard combines lost-wax casting with repoussé.

With Style v, which seems to coincide with the first century BC, the comparatively isolated development of British art comes to an end in southern England. In the second half of that century the neighbouring Gauls were under Roman control, and increasingly Britain was drawn into the same sphere. By Augustan times decorated Roman objects were in use and for the first time in the Iron Age there are undoubted imports from the Continent. In the north and in Scotland a distinctive art style continued to flourish, but workshops in the south of England copied Roman products, and British traditions were influenced by Roman taste.

3 Dress and jewellery

The Gauls are tall in stature and their flesh is very moist and white, while their hair is not only naturally blond, but they also use artificial means to increase this natural quality of colour. For they continually wash their hair with lime-wash and draw it back from the forehead to the crown and to the nape of the neck... the hair is so thickened by this treatment that it differs in no way from a horse's mane. Some shave off the beard, while others cultivate a short beard; the nobles shave the cheeks but let the moustache grow freely so that it covers the mouth.

DIODORUS SICULUS

30 *Right, above* Three cast bronze masks from Welwyn. Heights 39, 41 and 39mm.

31 *Far right* Although it is not a Celtic antiquity, this tattooed skin from a human arm, found in a contemporary grave in Siberia, illustrates an art form which might have been common in Celtic lands. Length 600mm.

The description by Diodorus Siculus provides an interesting contrast with the modern image of the short dark Celt and illustrates the dangers of generalisations which ignore chronology and geography. Caesar confirms that the Britons too 'wear their hair long, and shave the whole of their bodies except the head and upper lip'. Very few British skeletons have been studied, and most of them are from Yorkshire, but they suggest that men were on average 1.67m (5ft 6in) tall and women 1.56m (5ft 1½ in), whilst life expectancy was about thirty years, with only 3 per cent of the population over the age of forty-five. Representations of Britons include the bronze head on the North Grimston (N. Yorks.) 59 sword-hilt, and three bronze masks from a grave at Welwyn (Herts.): all have the hair 30 swept back from the face in accord with the descriptions, and the Welwyn heads also have long moustaches. Bronze razors are known in Hallstatt times, but there are no La Tène razors in Britain until the end of the first century BC, when large triangular 'razor-knives' were used. The shears with which they must have cut their hair are rarely found but there is a large pair from a grave at Hertford Heath (Herts.).

'All the Britons dye their bodies with woad, which produces a blue colour, and this gives them a more terrifying appearance in battle.' Caesar's observation is expanded by Herodian: 'they mark their bodies with various figures of all kinds of animals and wear no clothes for fear of concealing these figures'. Herodian was mistaken in thinking that they wore no clothes, although they might well have stripped for battle (p.50). The leaves of woad were an important source of blue dye until the first half of the present century, and the Britons evidently used it to paint or tattoo their bodies. No Briton's skin has

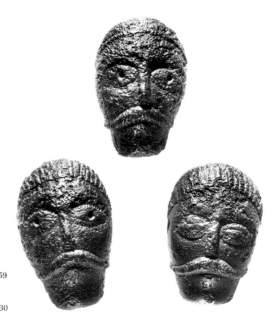

ever been found, tattooed, painted or plain, but the body of an Iron Age warrior completely preserved in Siberia's permafrost gives some idea of the scope of what 31 might have been a common British art form now completely lost.

According to Diodorus Siculus, the Gauls 'wear a striking kind of clothing – tunics dyed and stained in various colours, and trousers, which they call by the name of bracae; and they wear striped cloaks, fastened with buckles, thick in winter and light in summer, picked out with a variegated small check pattern'. Very occasionally fabric has been preserved – either in waterlogged conditions or where the structure of small pieces of cloth has been replaced by corrosion products from adjoining metal brooches.

But of the dress described by Diodorus Siculus the most that the archaeologist can expect to find is the buckle, or brooch, which fastened the cloak. Although there are Hallstatt brooches in Britain – types which are commonly found in Italy – not one comes from an undoubtedly ancient context and they may be comparatively recent imports. Certainly the Late Hallstatt brooches of types common in Gaul were rarely worn in Britain. But from about 400 BC La Tène brooches are fairly frequent: some were perhaps imported, though the vast majority must have been manufactured locally. Such brooches were usually bronze, and the prototypes were made in one piece. The decorative body would be cast; then a projection from the head would be hammered and drawn into a long wire to form the spring and pin. The spring was coiled first to the right of the brooch-bow and then to the left, always in the same way so that the pin was engaged in a catch-plate on the same side of the brooch. From the catch-plate extends a foot which turns back to the bow; both foot and bow are sometimes decorated in the original casting and occasionally, especially on the foot, provision is made for an applied bead of coral or 'enamel' inlay. Iron brooches were made to the same pattern, but were entirely forged and not cast. This type of brooch was popular for a couple of centuries, and then the design was improved by lengthening the free end of the foot, which was liable to get bent and broken, and clasping it to the bow with a separate collar. This development distinguishes the La Tène II brooch from La Tène I. It was then a short step, although it took about a century to achieve it, to cast or forge the bow and end of the foot together – this is the distinctive feature of the La Tène III brooch. This classic typological sequence 32 is used to distinguish the three stages of La Tène chronology, but it does not accommodate all La Tène brooches and Britain, in particular, has several peculiarities.

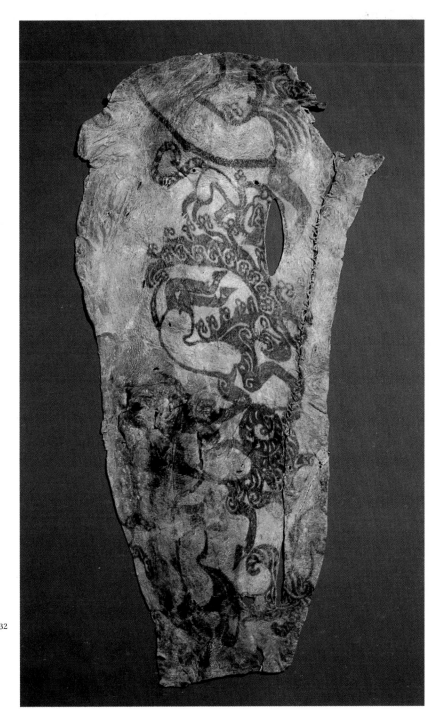

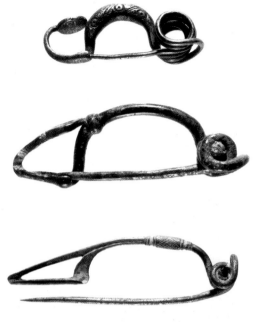

32 *Right* A typological sequence of British La Tène bronze brooches: I, Wood Eaton (Oxon.); II, Wetwang Slack (N. Humberside); III Unprovenanced. Lengths 47, 69 and 67mm.

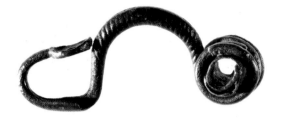

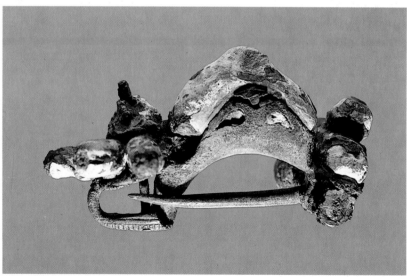

34 Bronze and coral brooch from the Queen's Barrow, Arras (see also 42). Length 66mm.

The manufacturers of British La Tène I brooches seem to have had difficulty in constructing the spring mechanism normal to the Continental brooch. Certainly some sprung brooches were made here, but the Britons also experimented with various forms of hinge mechanism. In one of the more popular forms the bow terminated in a single ring which superficially resembles the coil of a spring; the pin was manufactured separately with two linked 33 coils to fit on either side of that ring and the junction was secured by a rivet. Other British brooches had a pin simply pivoted between two projecting lugs. But the attachment of the pin was not the only British innovation, for at a comparatively early stage the foot was cast in one with the bow. This development, which distinguishes the La Tène III brooch on the Continent, is seen in the much earlier Queen's Barrow at Arras, where the brooch 34 is otherwise of La Tène I shape and has elaborate ornament suggesting influence from the La Tène I 'Münsingen' brooch on the Continent. Many British La Tène II bronze brooches have the foot and bow cast in one piece, although iron brooches were still made with a foot which had to be secured to the bow by a collar.

The distinctive 'involuted' brooch developed in Britain in La Tène II. The bows on some British brooches of La Tène I form were much flatter than those fashionable on the Continent, and it seems that the involuted brooch evolved from these. When 35

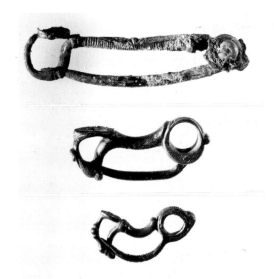

33 *Left* Bronze La Tène I brooch from Lakenheath (Suffolk), lacking the pin but showing the hollow cylindrical rivet linking two parts of an imitation spring. Length 49mm.

35 *Right* Sequence of bronze brooches illustrating the development of the involuted brooch. The one at the bottom is from Danes Graves and the other two are from Burton Fleming. Lengths 77, 48 and 36mm.

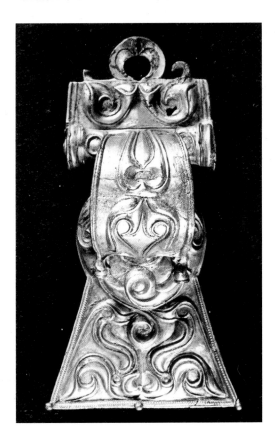

36 The Aesica brooch. Length 103mm.

securing the pin in its catch-plate it would be natural to press down on the centre of the bow, and a long flat bow could easily become down-curved, or involuted. Many brooches were deliberately manufactured in this way, and an interesting sequence of graves at Wetwang Slack (N. Humberside) has shown how the long involuted brooch was gradually superseded by a shorter and more curved variety. The involuted brooch had its heyday in the second century BC, but there is at the moment no means of knowing how much later it was used.

In the first century BC, and especially after Caesar's expeditions, British brooches again came under the influence of the Continental tradition. New forms may have been imported, perhaps including some of the silver brooches found in cemeteries in south-eastern England. Silver was never common with the Celts and these La Tène III pieces resemble Italian silver brooches – they were used at a time when other Italian imports were certainly reaching Britain. But other La Tène III brooches in Britain are sufficiently distinctive to show that there must have been a flourishing native industry. Brooches were now occasionally worn in pairs, sometimes linked by a chain, in a way known on the Continent since the fifth century BC. By the first century AD brooches of many types were in common use all over southern England: few of them have other than the simplest decoration, but occasionally an elaborate Celtic design is found. The most ornate is the surprisingly large gilt-bronze brooch from Aesica (the Latin **36** name for Great Chesters, Northumberland) found in a small hoard of jewellery in 1894. Records of the discovery are unsatisfactory, but the hoard seems to have been concealed at the end of the third century AD, although the brooch was probably made two hundred years earlier. 'Of its kind

37 *Right* A bronze pin with coral ornament, from Danes Graves. length 126mm.

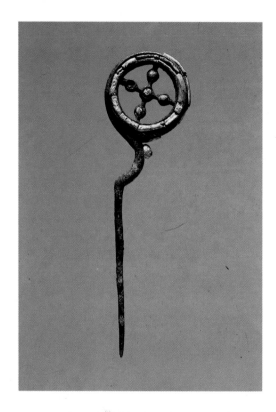

38 *Below* Bracelets from Cowlam (*centre front*) and Burton Fleming: the one on the left is made of jet (diameter 84mm) and the others are bronze (diameters *c.* 60mm).

probably the most fantastically beautiful creation that has come to us from antiquity', enthused Sir Arthur Evans – but to J. M. de Navarro it was 'rather flamboyant, not to say vulgar'.

The pin is a simpler form of dress fastening which seems to have been used throughout the Iron Age, although it was never particularly common. There were only four pins from the 446 burials at Wetwang Slack, two of them in one grave, and no site has produced more. The finest pins are quite long and have ornamental heads, often ring-heads, and a 'swan's neck' bend in the stem. Two ornate pins from the Yorkshire graves were found 37 immediately adjoining the skulls, suggesting that they may have been hair-pins, but because of the way in which the skeletons had been bundled up a dress fastening from the upper part of the body could easily have fallen by the skull.

After brooches bracelets were the most popular ornament, but whereas up to a 38

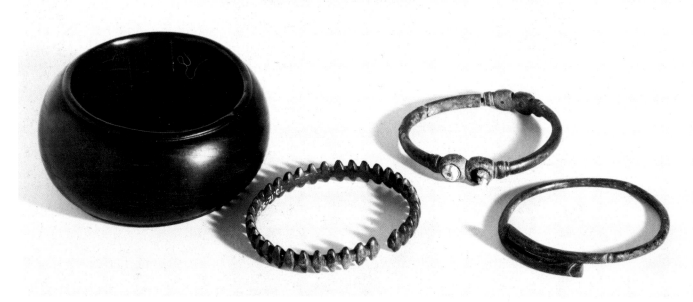

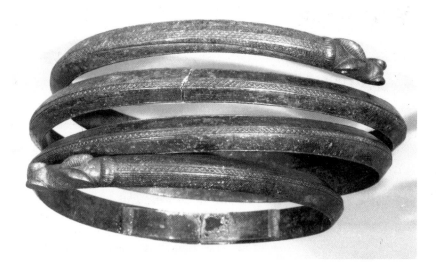

39 Bronze bracelet from Snailwell. Diameter 105mm.

40 Bronze armlets, one with enamel ornament, from Castle Newe (Aberdeenshire). Diameters 141 and 147mm.

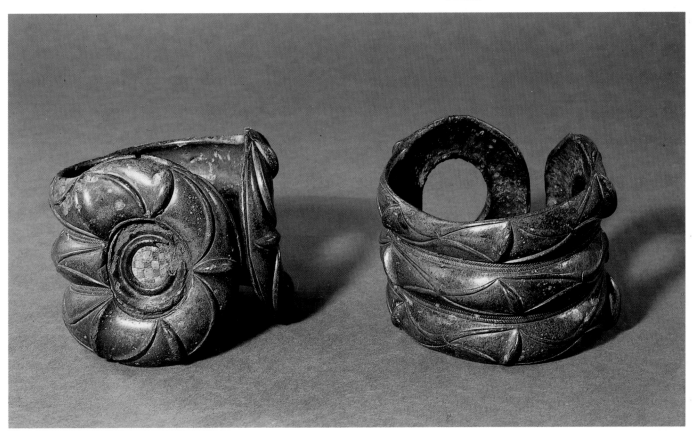

third of the Yorkshire burials had a brooch with them no more than 5 per cent had a bracelet. The finest bracelets were made of bronze and some had decorative settings for inlay. They fitted fairly closely round the wrist so various devices had to be used to allow them to be pushed over the hand: some had a simple opening in one side, others had a projection at one end of the break to fit in a hole at the other (a mortice-and-tenon fitting) and there was a third type with overlapping terminals. A few shale or jet bracelets have been found, and some made of iron belonged to the later stages of the Wetwang Slack cemetery. The bracelets in these Yorkshire cemeteries were always worn by women, but according to classical writers bracelets were worn by both men and women in Gaul. The cremation at Snailwell (Cambs.) seems to have been that of a male – certainly the grave-goods included a shield-boss and a razor-knife – and one of the finest objects found there was a spirally twisted bracelet with 'snake-head' terminals. This is the 39 only bracelet of its type from England, though there are others from Scotland. A related type is the 'massive armlet', found 40 only in Scotland and Ireland, cast by the lost-wax process and sometimes with enamel or glass ornament in the terminals. The decoration of the metalwork is consistent with other pieces from northern England and Scotland dating from the end of the first century and the second century AD. They have never been found on a skeleton and indeed these ungainly objects could perhaps have been intended for gods rather than men. Conceivably they could have been worn round the ankle. Anklets were certainly worn on the Continent and one is supposed to have been found on one of the Arras skeletons.

In the Wetwang Slack cemetery more

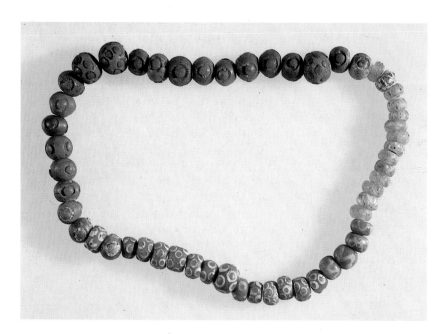

than 500 glass beads were found, most of them in 10 different necklaces: 80 per cent of the beads were plain and only 6 per cent contained colours other than blue. Three other Yorkshire skeletons had bead necklaces, including one from Cowlam which has one large bead decorated with inset white rings and 69 with white scrolls. White ornament on a blue base was popular and circles were created either by insetting annulets in channelled rings or by inserting a white disc in a hollow and superimposing a central blue dot ('stratified eye bead'). All the types of beads found so far in Yorkshire are represented in the necklace from the Queen's Barrow at Arras, 41 including translucent beads with a greenish tinge decorated with white or yellow scrolls. Of the 100 beads said to have originally made up the necklace, 67 still survive.

The majority of the Yorkshire burials are without grave-goods and the rest are but poorly equipped. The Queen's Barrow

41 Necklace of glass beads from the Queen's Barrow, Arras (see also 42).

group, however, is comparatively rich and is worth listing. Found in 1816 in a shallow grave under a small barrow, the skeleton had been adorned with the necklace of glass beads, an amber ring, bronze and coral brooch (34), two bronze bracelets, a bronze and coral pendant or belt-fitting and a gold finger-ring – the only Celtic gold ring from Britain now, unfortunately, lost. Finger-rings of any metal are rare; curiously, toe-rings seem to have been more common.

A type of object often associated with the Celts is the torque; it is mentioned several times by classical writers, is shown on representations, and found in graves. The torque is a collar, or neck-ring, and its name comes from one of the more common varieties, the hoop of which is a twisted strand of metal: a Roman, T. Manlius, took a collar from a Celtic warrior and earned himself the cognomen of Torquatus. At the Battle of Telemon 'all the warriors in the front ranks were adorned in gold necklaces and bracelets' (Polybius) – and that was not an isolated occurrence. But in Celtic graves torques are usually associated with women rather than warriors, and are made of bronze, rarely of iron, but hardly ever of gold. On the Continent they are best known from graves in Champagne, where they were extremely popular until La Tène II, but then they became rare and they are never found with La Tène III burials.

In Britain torques are virtually absent from graves. The Yorkshire inhumations have bead necklaces instead, and the La Tène III cremations in south-eastern England resemble contemporary cremations in northern France and the Rhineland and have no torques. But their absence from graves does not mean that they were not worn by some of the Britons, for there is a rich collection of material – often gold – from other sources. Gold torques must have been valuable always, and thus vulnerable: when they were broken, damaged or unfashionable they would have been melted down, and it is hardly surprising that they are not found in graves. They found their way into the metalsmith's crucible in recent as well as ancient times: the surviving fragments from Clevedon (Avon) are the remains of a find made before 1897 and 'mostly melted by Parson & Son, Bristol'. A most unusual burial was said to have been found at Mildenhall (Suffolk) in 1812 – 'a human skeleton of large dimensions, stretched at its full

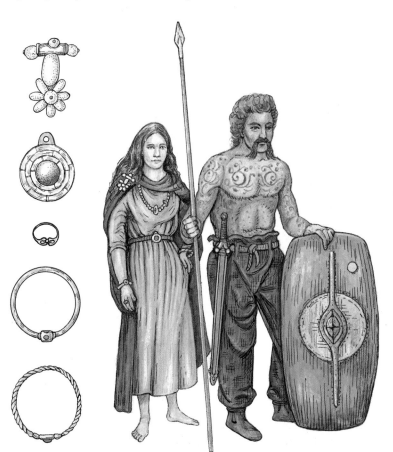

42 A British lady and warrior, equipped with items found in the graves in the Queen's Barrow, Arras, and at Grimthorpe. Some of the Queen's Barrow jewellery is shown in detail on the left; for the brooch see also 34, and the necklace 41. For the roundel on the Grimthorpe shield see 74. (From a painting by Philip Compton.)

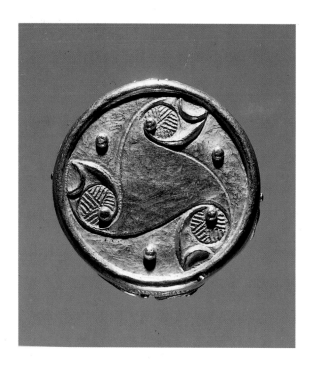

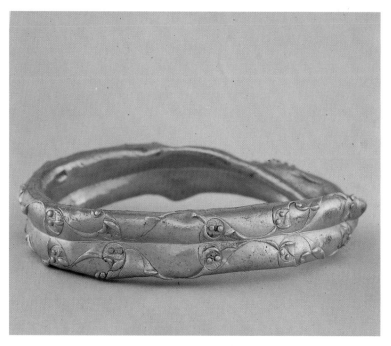

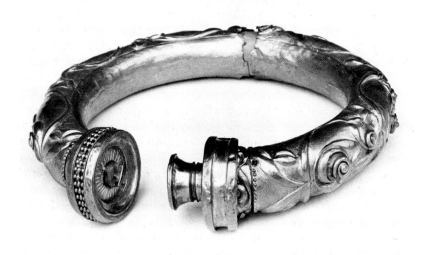

length between the skeletons of two horses... on one side of the warrior lay a long iron sword, on the other his celt: he had a torque of gold' – but the torque was immediately melted down by a silversmith at Bury St Edmunds.

The gold torques that do survive, however, are very impressive. One found at Broighter (Co. Derry) in 1896 is a magnificent piece of work which has a somewhat chequered history. Found by a ploughman with a curious assemblage of other gold objects – two torques of different types, a model boat, a bowl and two fine chain necklaces – it was bought by the British Museum but then claimed as Treasure Trove by the Royal Irish Academy. A famous trial at the Royal Courts of Justice in London in 1903 decided in favour of the Irish and the collection is now exhibited at Dublin. Subsequently one reputable archaeologist claimed that the hoard had

44

43 *Far left* The terminal of the Clevedon torque, with a triskele motif (Style v). Diameter 34mm.

44 *Bottom left* Gold torque from Broighter. Diameter 195mm.

45 *Left* Gold bracelet from Snettisham (Style v). Diameter 97mm.

been collected and buried in the nineteenth century, and another declared that it had been found in an old umbrella in a ditch! But the authenticity of the association is now generally accepted, and there is no doubt at all that the torque is a genuine La Tène antiquity. It is made of two hollow tubes with linked terminals – the swivel-joint can be opened by turning one half through 90° – and there must have been a decorative 'muff' to secure the two ends at the back. The rich chased decoration (not repoussé) seems to have been executed before the tubes were shaped. The high-relief 'snail-shells' have been separately applied, and the background to the design has been covered by fine arcs for which the compass-points can still be distinguished.

Three rather similar but less ornate tubular torques, one large and two small, were found with the remains of a fourth torque in a field at Snettisham (Norfolk) in 1948. Each had a tubular body, made in two halves like the Broighter torque, with buffer terminals and a band to cover the joint at the back. That field at Snettisham produced five hoards in the course of deep-ploughing in the autumns of 1948 and 1950: four of them were within 25m of one another and the fifth was about 55m away. Subsequently four more torques were found in three different parts of the field in the course of agricultural work. In total there are the remains of at least sixty-one torques (including fragments which may have been from bracelets), two bracelets and 158 coins, as well as rings and other fragments including lumps of tin and gold obtained from melting down other objects. Many of the objects were made of gold, or electrum, and the whole collection may have been buried simultaneously in the second half of the first century BC. If it is to be treated as an entity, then it seems likely that it was the stock of a metalworker who dispersed his holding for safe-keeping, but if this is the correct interpretation then the owner had carefully sorted his treasure. Different types of torque were found in each hoard: hoard A had tubular torques only; B and C, muddled together after the ploughing, produced at least forty-eight torques or bracelets with twisted hoops and loop terminals – on excavation the only three multi-strand buffer terminal torques were found in C. The only complete gold-alloy loop-terminal torque came from D, and E produced a magnificent multi-strand torque with ring terminals, as well as part of a twisted torque with buffer terminals, and a unique 45 bracelet.

The multi-strand torque from hoard E, now known as the Snettisham torque, is 46 one of Britain's finest antiquities. Its hoop is made of eight strands twisted together, and each strand in turn comprises eight lengths of swaged wire twisted together. The ends of the wires have been secured in terminals made by the lost-wax process. The decoration on the terminals, which would have been modelled in the wax, is formed by low-relief lobes, some of which define voids of distinctive Style v shape with matted hatching. Details, including the small knobs with triple dots, show a close relationship with the terminal of a similar torque from nearby Sedgeford and more surprisingly with a comparable terminal from Cairnmuir in Scotland. A small Gaulish coin trapped within the Snettisham torque (but not necessarily deliberately concealed by the manufacturer, as originally reported) is of the same type as the coins in hoard B and supports the notion that all the hoards are more or less contemporary.

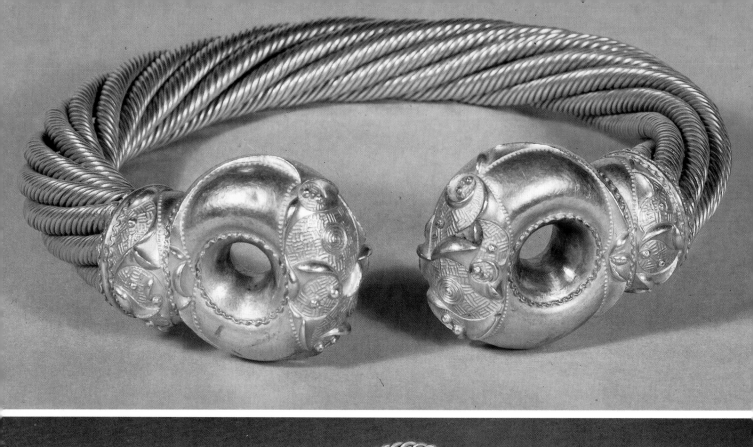
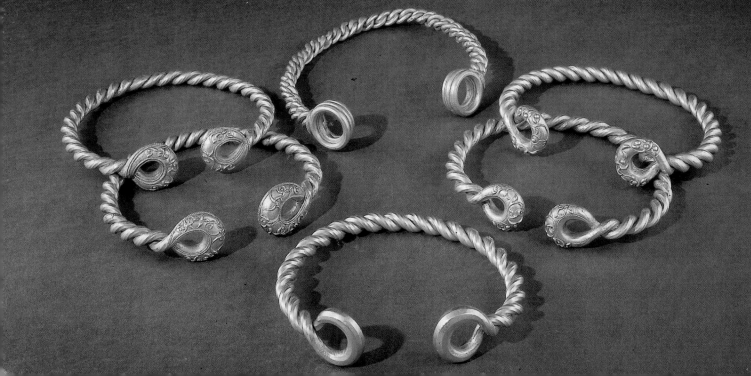

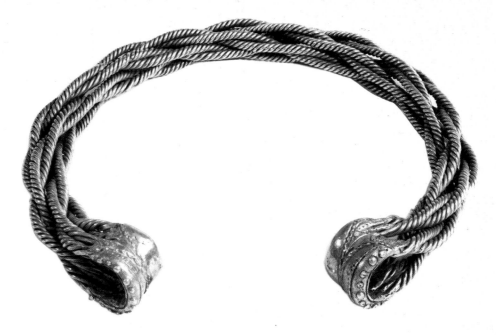

48 *Right* Gold torque from Needwood Forest. Diameter 179mm.

46 *Left* The Snettisham torque (Style v). Diameter 199mm.

47 *Left* The Ipswich torques (Style v). Diameters 181 to 197mm. See also contents page.

A hoard of five torques was found at Ipswich (Suffolk) in 1968, when a machine was moving earth on a new housing estate: a sixth torque found two years later in a nearby garden may have been displaced from the original hoard. They were made of a gold alloy (on average 80 per cent gold) and all had twisted hoops and ring terminals: nos 1 – 5 are quite similar, but no. 6 is different – and it may be no coincidence that the slightly different torque was found apart – as at Snettisham. Torque no. 1 had plain terminals; nos 2 – 5 had relief designs like those on the Snettisham torque, but without the hatched surfaces. Experiments showed how these torques could have been constructed: from a cast ingot a long faceted wire was formed; that was bent in half and the two strands twisted together; the terminals were then cast-on using the lost-wax process. Torques nos 4 and 5 were left 'as cast' from the mould, but nos 2 and 3 were worked over with a tracer which has obscured most of the tool-marks modelled in the wax. The sixth Ipswich torque had ring-terminals cast-on to a hoop made by twisting together two pairs of gold wires.

East Anglia is not the only source of gold torques, for two of a rather different type were found within 25km of one another at Glascote and Needwood Forest, in Staffordshire. Both have multi-strand hoops onto which somewhat similar broad loop terminals have been cast: they resemble a torque from Ulceby (S. Humberside) and like all surviving gold torques in England they should date from the first century BC. But torques were still used in the middle of the following century, according to the description of Queen Boudicca given by Dio Cassius: 'in stature she was very tall, in appearance most terrifying, in the glance of her eye most fierce, and her voice was harsh; a great mass of the tawniest hair fell to her hips; around her neck was a large golden necklace'.

4 Hearth and home

Their houses are large and circular, built of planks and wickerwork, the roof being a dome of heavy thatch.

STRABO

Strabo's description of a Gallic house might well be applied to Britain – indeed, on present evidence it suits Britain better than Gaul – but such structures leave little trace for the archaeologist. Remains of domestic architecture are restricted to plans of circular huts usually from 5 to 9m in diameter, but some up to 15m, in the form of a ring of post-holes or a rough stone foundation course, and the only refinements are the occasional porch and a trench to divert rainwater. Very occasionally finds add a touch of colour, as in the hillfort at Hod Hill (Dorset), where some huts had collections of sling-stones, presumably once in bags, stored ready for action by the doorway, and one hut thought to belong to a chieftain had a spearhead in a similar position. Perhaps the buildings were decorated inside with fabric wall-hangings, but these and any other fitments have long since perished and significant artefacts are limited to the latch-lifter that opened the door. Of furniture there was probably very little: in Gaul 'when dining they all sit not in chairs, but on the earth' and 'their custom is to sleep on the ground upon the skins of wild animals' (Diodorus Siculus). Animal skins must include those of the brown bear, because two cremations in southern England produced terminal phalanges – the claws that would have been left in a treated skin.

The Gauls dined next to 'hearths blazing with fire, with cauldrons and spits containing large pieces of meat' (Diodorus Siculus); here metal artefacts come more into the picture. Iron fire-dogs are known especially from graves in south-eastern England, a ritual deposition that gives no idea of their original distribution. They may well have been used in pairs like their recent counterparts, and were possibly intended to

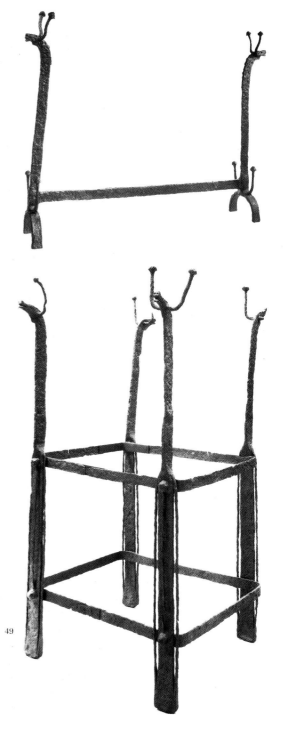

49

49 *Left* Iron fire-dog from Welwyn. Height 970/985mm.

51 *Right* Hand-made decorated pottery from Somerset: a jar (height 355mm) and a bowl from Meare and a lid from Glastonbury.

50 *Left* Iron frame from Welwyn. Height 1.43m.

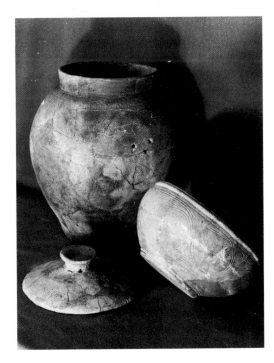

contain the logs of the fire. The Iron Age hearth was in the centre of the room, not against the wall, so the fire-dogs could be viewed from all sides and they therefore had a head at each end. Their exceptionally long necks have never been satisfactorily explained: an elaborate example from Capel Garmon (Gwynedd) has loops at either end of the uprights which could have held cross-bars to support spits, but no other fire-dog has such attachments. A curious iron frame found in a La Tène III 50 grave at Welwyn (Herts.) looks like a pair of fire-dogs linked together and has two tiers of cross-struts. Perhaps it was used as a brazier, although it would have needed gridded walls and floor; certainly it should in some way be connected with a fire. Several bronze cauldrons are known, and a grave at Stanfordbury (Beds.) included an iron tripod from which a cauldron had been suspended.

Throughout the British Iron Age jars and bowls were made of pottery. Many of them must have been made in the home, but some of the finer wares were produced professionally and traded. Decoration is usually unambitious but some of the professional products have incised scrolls and 51 curvilinear patterns with shapes infilled with hatching. After Caesar's expeditions to Britain trade with Gaul was increased and fine table-ware came on to the British market.

Italian wine was imported from the end of the second century BC, in tall pottery amphorae, found in sherds on settlements 52 and sometimes complete in graves. Diodorus Siculus reported that the Gauls were 'exceedingly fond of wine and sate themselves with the unmixed wine imported by merchants; their desire makes them drink it greedily and when they become drunk they fall into a stupor or into a maniacal disposition'. Doubtless the Britons were affected in the same way, but as time went on they adopted some of the refinements of the Romans. The new drink could be better appreciated in an Italian silver cup: several were imported towards the end of the first century BC, and half a dozen survive. But British metalworkers did not attempt to copy them. The principal native drinking-vessel of the time was the tankard, made of wood and banded with bronze, furnished with a cast bronze handle, and better suited to native beer. Merchants provided those who preferred wine with the means of serving it: not only a bronze jug but also a long-handled pan in which it could be warmed. The Roman drinking service would not have been complete without a bucket in which the wine was mixed, but it seems that this item was not

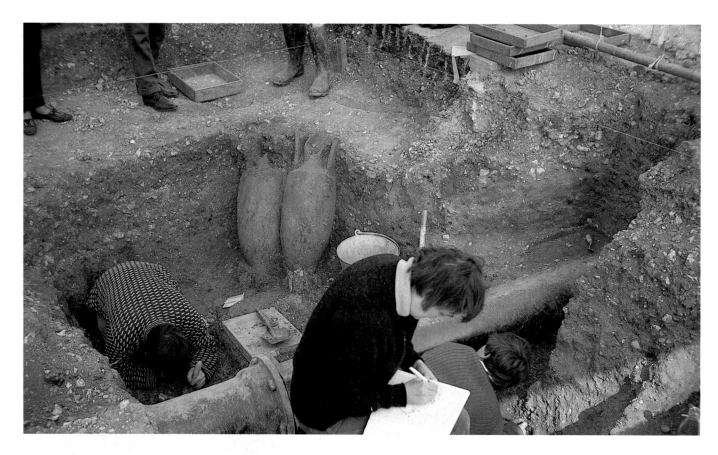

52 The excavation of a rich La Tène III burial at Welwyn Garden City in 1965. A gas-pipe trench had destroyed part of the grave but most of the grave-goods were recovered and a complete plan was reconstructed. The grave measured 3.2 by 2.2m and contained five amphorae, two of which were still in position when this photograph was taken. For glass game-pieces from this burial see 93.

traded to Britain. In a grave at Aylesford (Kent) an imported bronze jug and pan were accompanied by a Celtic bronze-bound wooden bucket whose final use had been as the depository for the cremated bones. A pair of comparable vessels from a grave at Baldock (Herts.) was associated with an Italian amphora, and it is tempting to see the type as the native equivalent of a wine-mixing bucket. The Aylesford grave was discovered in a gravel pit in 1886 and shown to Arthur Evans, who was visiting the site with his father in search of Stone Age implements. It had not been excavated under the best of circumstances, but the rim, uppermost bronze band, internal

bronze band, handle-mounts and handle held together in one piece, with fragments of wooden staves trapped between the bronze bands. The arrangement of the lower part of the bucket is not so certain, but on the strength of a tiny decorated fragment and on the analogy of the Baldock buckets (excavated under even more unfortunate circumstances, by a bulldozer) it can be equipped with three feet. The bronze-bound iron handle pivots in holes in the back of two cast bronze handle-mounts, each in the form of a helmeted human head; these had been dismantled and reattached twice, suggesting some antiquity for the bucket before it was

53

buried. The upper band has relief ornament produced in formers (see p.8), and the most interesting design is a pair of confronted animals based on horses, or perhaps stags, created by an artist not unduly worried by details of anatomy. These fantastic animals have antlers, curling lips, bifurcating devil-like tails, and human knees. At Marlborough (Wilts.) a cremation was found in a far grander vessel, which had capacity of about eight times that of the Aylesford bucket. It was

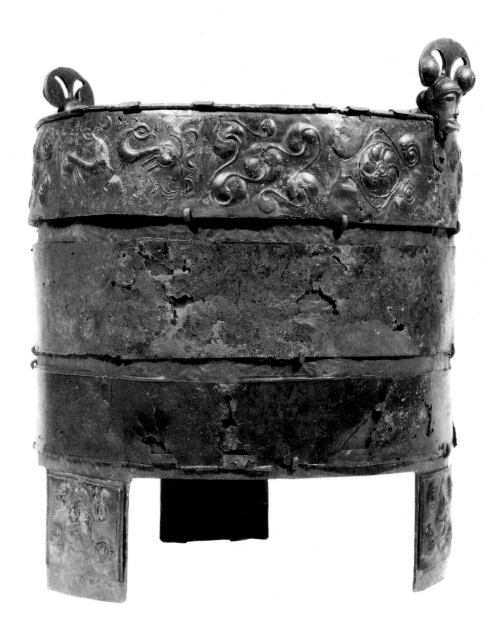

53 The Aylesford bucket; for a detail of the animals on the upper band see 6. Height (excluding the helmeted handle-mounts) 300mm.

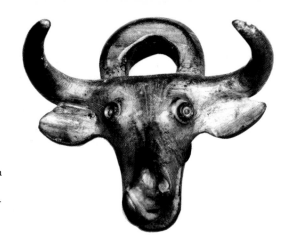

54 A cow licking its muzzle, a bronze escutcheon from a bucket, found at Felmersham. The span of the horns is 46mm.

recorded and lifted by the Rev. Charles Francis about 1807 – a 'drawing was made on the spot while it was entire', but 'it would not bear the smallest jar or shake, and it fell to pieces'. According to the original drawing there were three decorated bands, but only fragments survive.

The Aylesford burial dates from the second half of the first century BC and there is no reason to doubt that the Marlborough bucket was contemporary with it. The three Welwyn heads (30), too, are from a grave that dates from the very end of that century, and there are few earlier representations of humans or deities. The head on the North Grimston sword is usually 59 dated in the second century BC, and a face peering from the Torrs horns (p.64) is certainly earlier than the Aylesford bucket, but these pieces are exceptional. Fantastic animals have been seen on sword scabbards of the third century BC and there are faces in the designs of the Wandsworth 75 mask shield and the Witham shield (which also once carried a long-legged boar), but 3 fairly naturalistic renderings of animals, too, are rare before the first century BC.

From Felmersham (Beds.) comes a pair of handle-mounts in the form of cows' heads. They were cast by the lost-wax process and each is slightly different from the other: the difference is quite deliberate in that only one of the cows' heads has an 5 outstretched tongue licking its muzzle. From the back of the casting projects a stout rivet to attach it to a wooden bucket, and on top of the head is a ring to take the end of the bucket's handle. There are several other bovine handle fittings, and Fox suggested that they might have belonged to milk pails: all the more reason for the helmeted heads from Aylesford and Baldock to have presided over a much more formidable brew. There are few representations of animals other than cows and bulls, but a fine pair of heads with rams' horns – also bucket escutcheons – 5 was found in what seems to have been a disturbed grave at Harpenden (Herts.). They are powerfully modelled, each with hollow oval eyes perhaps once inlaid with 'enamel', a long bony snout and large circular settings for 'enamel' at the nostrils, sides of the mouth and perhaps at the back of the head as well.

Classical writers speak of the vanity of the Celts, and Strabo comments on the beauty of the women. Their houses may not have been equipped with much in the way of furniture, but at least they had the luxury of admiring themselves in mirrors. Three Yorkshire graves produced mirrors of iron, but in the south magnificent decorated bronze mirrors were fashionable 5 towards the end of the first century BC. Most known mirrors come from graves, so information about their development is patchy, depending on chance survival in the cremation burials of south-eastern England. The mirror was a luxury item, offering scope for decoration not only in its cast handle but also, more importantly, on the flat field of the mirror-plate itself. The viewing surface was polished and plain, but its back was often covered with elabo-

55 A ram's head, a bronze escutcheon from a bucket, found at Harpenden. Height 75mm.

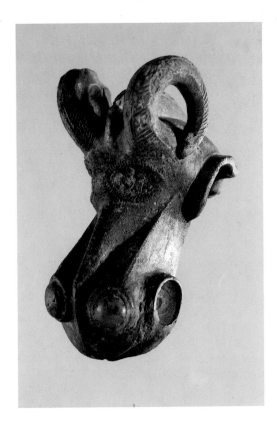

rate line-work; when not in use it may well have been hung on the wall, in which case the decorated side would normally have been seen with the handle at the top.

Mirror decoration was studied and perceptively analysed by Sir Cyril Fox, who saw the development of the decoration in terms of a typological sequence evolved from the triskele within a circle as seen on the Llyn Cerrig Bach repoussé plaque (28). The designs were sometimes enclosed in two or three adjoining circles; more often the circles merged into a scroll but a tripartite arrangement could be distinguished in all but the most devolved examples. Fox saw 'a familiar evolution of art forms' spanning less than a century: 'if Mayer [56a] may be regarded as archaic,

Colchester with its severe and regular structure [56b] is classic; Birdlip [56c] may be held to correspond to the 'decorated' phase of medieval, the 'baroque' phase of renaissance art; Desborough [57] is clearly to be defined as 'flamboyant', less justly perhaps as 'rococo'.' But he treated his sequence too seriously when it came to assigning dates, suggesting limits of AD 5 – 20 for the Great Chesterford mirror (56f) and AD 1 – 15 for the one from Colchester (56b). In fact none of the mirrors can be dated closely, because none has particularly useful associations, but most seem to belong to the century after Caesar's expeditions.

Detailed study of the construction of the designs, by a team led by Richard Savage, has enabled the marks of various tools to be identified. Only on the Mayer mirror was the standard of craftsmanship so high that it was impossible to tell whether the design had been chased or engraved. The Mayer design was constructed with compasses, but free-hand scratched 'guide-lines' can be distinguished, and it is difficult to understand their function. Some of the work, as on the Holcombe mirror, was meticulous and time-consuming, but other examples, such as Old Warden, have uneven outlines and rough hatching carried out quickly using a tool with a broken edge. From a technical point of view the mirrors seem to group geographically, with a series of related pieces along the Jurassic belt from Devon via Gloucestershire to Northamptonshire, and a second group to the south-east from Buckinghamshire and Bedfordshire across to Essex. Detailed study of the marks of tools is an approach which falls short of identifying the work of individual craftsmen, but it reveals a great deal about the construction and execution of designs.

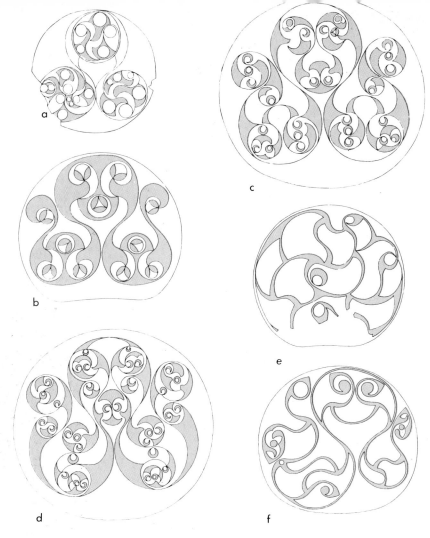

56 Decoration on the backs of
bronze mirrors (Style v):
a) Mayer Collection;
b) Colchester; c) Birdlip;
d) Holcombe; e) Old Warden;
f) Great Chesterford.

57 The Desborough
mirror (Style v). Length
350mm.

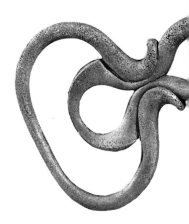

   The decorated mirror is one of the highlights of Celtic art, and a development which seems to be entirely insular. The Yorkshire iron mirrors may be compared with some from Celtic lands abroad, but the Continent has nothing to match the decorated bronze mirrors. In some of the symmetry, as on the Desborough mirror, Roman influence may be suspected, but other designs are far removed from classical taste. Such is Old Warden, with an overall network of distinctively shaped voids, and Great Chesterford, which Jope describes so vividly that we are obliged for ever to see it through his eyes: 'an unsteady lurch and a leering face, with wicked eyes running straight out into blunt-pointed ears, and spidery arms like tentacles wandering crazily through the available space to end in keeled-volute derivatives that look like ghoulish suckers'. One wonders how the British craftsman would have described his design, and indeed which way up he would have viewed it, if that mattered to him.

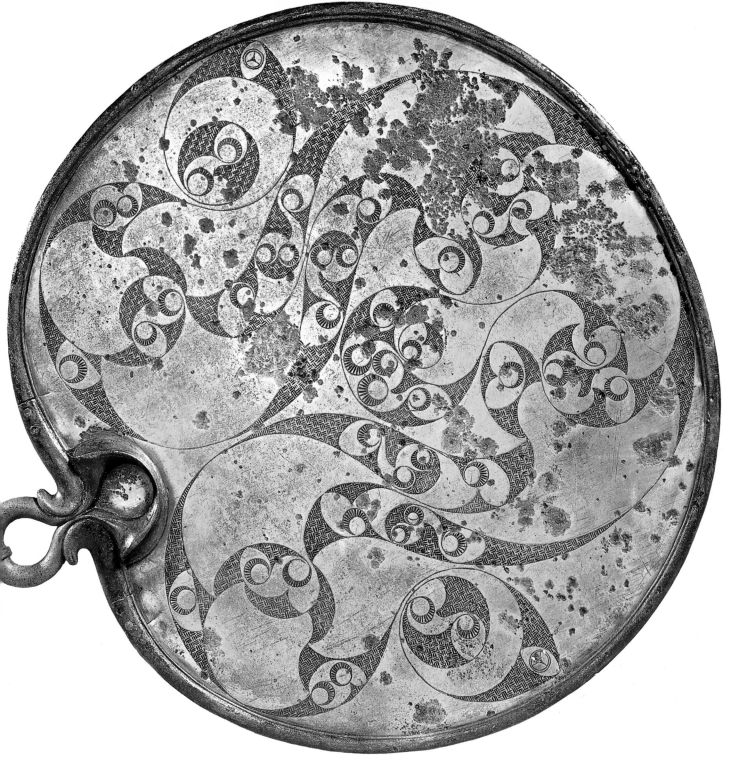

5 Weapons and armour

The whole race, which is now called Gallic or Galatic, is madly fond of war, high-spirited and quick to battle...

STRABO

Celtic warriors were armed with spears and swords, wore helmets and defended themselves with shields. Reconstruction drawings are well known, and usually such warriors wear the unique Thames helmet and carry the one and only Battersea shield. In order to establish the warrior's equipment, and to see how it varied from man to man, time to time and place to place, archaeologists rely on representations, historical accounts and collections of grave-goods – but for Britain information on all these scores is sadly defective.

On the Continent in the Late Hallstatt period and at the beginning of La Tène I it seems that the spear was the most popular weapon, sometimes accompanied by a dagger or short sword, and in places they also used the occasional battle-axe and bow and arrow. The long sword was introduced in La Tène I, and by La Tène II times warriors seem to have been regularly equipped with a single spear or lance, a long sword and a shield. In Britain there are only a few burials of armed warriors and most of them seem to belong to La Tène III, so it is impossible to generalise about changes in equipment. The burials at Grimthorpe (N. Humberside) and Owslebury (Hants.) have the standard trio of Continental La Tène II arms – sword, spear and shield – and one from Great Brackstead (Essex) has an additional spear. Otherwise associated weapons from graves include two swords and a shield from North Grimston (N. Yorks.); a sword and spear from Whitcombe (Dorset) and from five graves at Burton Fleming (N. Humberside), and a sword with no fewer than seven spears in another Burton Fleming grave. Whilst inhumations of warriors were accompanied by what seems to have been a working set of weapons, with cremations it was sometimes the practice to make do with only a representative object, or indeed part of an object: the rich Snailwell (Cambs.) burial, for instance, included an iron shield-boss which had been deliberately removed from the shield. No other weapon was found but it may well be that the boss was intended to indicate the dead man's status as a warrior. One weapon commonly used by the Britons but never found in graves is the sling: hoards of sling-stones have been excavated in several British hillforts.

Spears figure prominently in accounts of the Celts in battle, are the only weapons mentioned in Caesar's description of his invasion of Britain, and are sometimes depicted on British coins. The remains are limited to the iron missile-head, and it is usually impossible to determine whether the weapon had been a spear or javelin to be thrown, or a lance to be thrust. Most spearheads were simply forged from iron, but very occasionally they are decorated either with engraved or chased ornament or even with the addition of bronze. Quite exceptional is a decorated iron spearhead 58 found in the River Thames at London. On each side a bronze cut-out shape with chased decoration has been riveted to each wing: the four shapes and their ornament are all slightly different. It is hard to believe that this weapon would have been thrown at the enemy and it is more likely to have been the head of a chieftain's ceremonial spear.

Daggers and swords were doubtless more prestigious weapons – they were certainly more complex objects to make. As on the Continent, daggers were used in Late Hallstatt times and at the very beginning of La Tène I, but in the fourth century BC their place is taken by the long sword, the arrival of which presumably indicates a change in warriors' tactics. The La Tène I

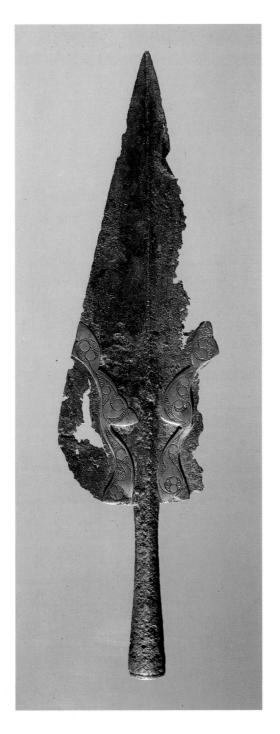

58 Iron spearhead with bronze decoration (Style V), from the River Thames. Length 302mm.

sword in Britain has a blade between 500 and 650mm long, which tapers in the final third of its length to a longish sharp point and was adapted equally well to cutting and thrusting. It may have been used in Britain well into La Tène II for the only scabbards with Style IV ornament (pp.20–1) are of this length.

The La Tène II sword was introduced at different times in different parts of Europe, but it seems to have been rare in Britain, where it is not readily distinguishable from the La Tène III sword. One example was found with a burial at North Grimston (N. Yorks): it has a long blade with very little taper and must have been used for slashing rather than thrusting. That burial is especially notable because it produced a second weapon, a very short sword with an exceptionally fine bronze hilt which figures a man's head – one of the very few representations of a Celt to be found in Britain. Such short swords with anthropomorphic hilts were used as accessory weapons throughout the La Tène period in all Celtic lands.

The length of the North Grimston long sword puts it in a class of its own in the north of England, where it alone exceeds the length of a La Tène I sword. Otherwise in the north later Iron Age swords differed only slightly in shape from the La Tène I blades, in that they usually lacked the distinctive taper, but were always relatively short. The La Tène III sword in the south of England resembles that used on the Continent: the blade is very long, from 700 to 900mm, has hardly any taper and was used exclusively for striking. The very marked difference between swords in the north and south suggests the parochial nature of contacts and conflicts in tribal Britain.

Swords themselves were rarely and only very simply decorated, but scabbards and

59

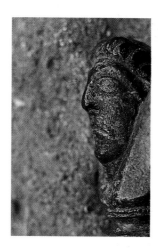

59 Head on the bronze hilt of a sword from North Grimston. Height of the head (to the chin) 28mm.

sheaths offered much more scope. The earliest dagger-sheaths were made of wood, sometimes wrapped with strips of bronze and sealed at the bottom with a ferrule, but most British Late Hallstatt sheaths were made entirely of metal. They have two shaped plates – a bronze front-plate (often decorated), the edges of which are wrapped round an iron back-plate, which has a suspension-loop towards the top. The tip of the two plates is secured at the bottom by a chape, which gave further scope for decoration. The chape was also subject to an interesting typological development. At first it was tubular, terminating in an anchor-like form; then the vulnerable projecting arms of the anchor were curved back and attached to the bottom of the sheath to form an open ring-like ending. The very fine cast chape from Wandsworth stands aside from this sequence, although its decoration and that of the sheath is quite in keeping with the Hallstatt tradition.

When they are decorated Late Hallstatt and La Tène I sheaths have simple geometric motifs, such as lozenges, triangles and sometimes compass-drawn arcs and circles down the borders of the front-plate. The position and form of some of this ornament suggests that the inspiration came from stitching along the sides of leather sheaths.

Scabbards, used to house the long sword introduced in La Tène I, may well have been made of wood or leather, but most known examples are of metal. Like the earlier sheaths, they were made of two plates, and their ends are clasped by a chape in the form of a frame, the top of which is bridged at the back and clamped on at the front. Few La Tène I iron scabbards are decorated, but one has chased decoration down the edges in the Late

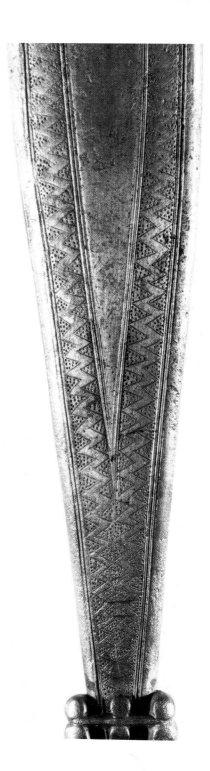

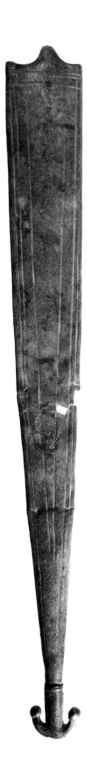
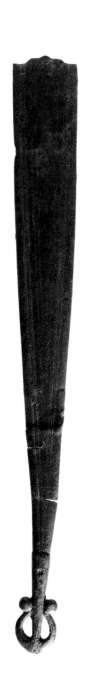
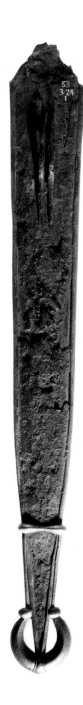
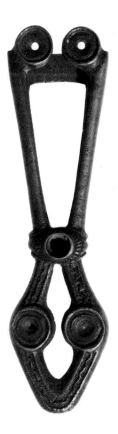

62 *Above* Cast bronze La Tène I chape from the north of Ireland. Length 104mm.

61 *Far left* Geometric decoration on the front-plate of a La Tène I bronze sheath from Richmond.

60 *Left* Dagger sheaths from the River Thames, showing a typological sequence of Late Hallstatt (*left* and *centre*) and La Tène I (*right*) chapes: *left*, Chelsea: *centre*, Barn Elms; *right*, Wandsworth. Full lengths 341, 295, and 312mm.

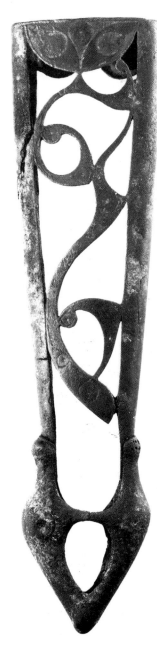

Hallstatt fashion and there are two from the Thames decorated with dragon-pairs (p.19) and a related piece from Fovant (Wilts.) (p.20) with Style IV decoration.

In England there are two scabbards with bronze parts decorated in Style IV: the magnificent Witham scabbard (24) and a bronze chape from Little Wittenham 63 (Oxon.), the back of which sports a cut-out design of tendrils with 'triangular' swellings and line-work fillings. There is, however, an interesting group of bronze scabbards from Ireland, four dredged from the River Bann and four more from a bog at Lisnacrogher (Co. Antrim): six of them are elaborately decorated down the full length of the front-plate. The only earlier scabbard-plate with overall decoration, also of bronze, is one from a Wisbech collection (18) with a sequence of s-motifs along the length of its front-plate. The design on one of the Lisnacrogher scabbards could be 64 interpreted as a development of the same theme, with a row of paired s-motifs, alternatively facing and backing – their terminals not linked but adjoining, and with something like an exploded palmette between each pair. The overall effect is of balanced waves and symmetrical tendrils, but in the filling of the upper tendrils there is no attempt at symmetry, with spirals, lobes, dots, concentric fillings and hatching all mixed together. This Lisnacrogher scabbard has an open chape-end of La Tène I form, and all the other Irish scabbards have closely similar chapes.

A scabbard-plate from the River Bann has a design much further removed from 65 symmetry, although a regular overall wave can be distinguished. Tightly coiled spirals figure large and spring from peltae and s-shapes which convolute to fill every available space. The infillings are varied and the borders have bands of geometric

63 Sheet bronze chape from Little Wittenham, with cut-out and engraved Style IV decoration and a cast-on chape-end. Length 165mm.

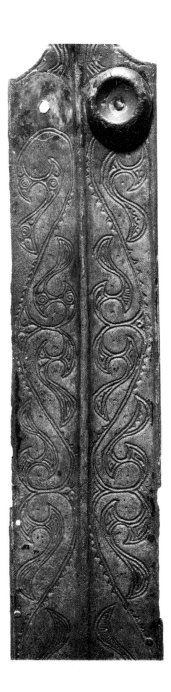

64 Style IV decoration on a bronze scabbard-plate from Lisnacrogher. Width 41mm.

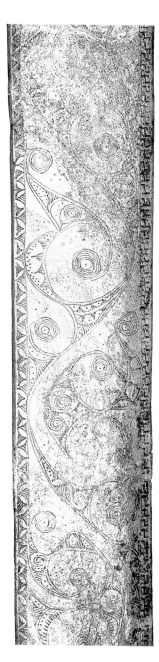

ornament which look back to the Hallstatt tradition, again via Wisbech.

The La Tène III sword in Yorkshire must usually have been housed in wooden or leather scabbards which left no trace, but an exception from Bugthorpe (N. Humberside) was in a scabbard with overall Style V ornament on the bronze front-plate and a badly corroded iron back-plate. In contrast, bronze La Tène III scabbards are relatively common in the south, and some very fine decorated examples are known. One found in 1982 at Little Wittenham (Oxon.) is in excellent condition: decorated with repoussé ornament in the top panel – featuring the Llyn Cerrig Bach trumpet shapes and voids of Style V – it also has fine chased 'laddering' for the length of the scabbard at either side of the central rib and cast relief ornament on the chape. Related scabbards have panels of engraved or chased ornament at the top. A quite different La Tène III type is represented by the bronze scabbard found at Isleham (Cambs.) in 1976. Engraved or inscribed ornament – again Style V – in panels at the top and bottom of the front plate is in near-pristine condition and the scabbard must have been nearly new when it was dropped, or thrown, into the River Lark. It has a squared instead of campanulate mouth, a rounded tip without a chape, and on the back its suspension-loop has an appendage stretching the full length of the scabbard: others of this type have been found in both the Witham and the Thames.

The Isleham sword, removed from its scabbard in the laboratory, proved to be in very poor condition, but towards the top of the blade was an armourer's mark. How far a craftsman specialised as an armourer rather than as a general blacksmith is unknown, but certainly the production of swords must have been a highly skilled

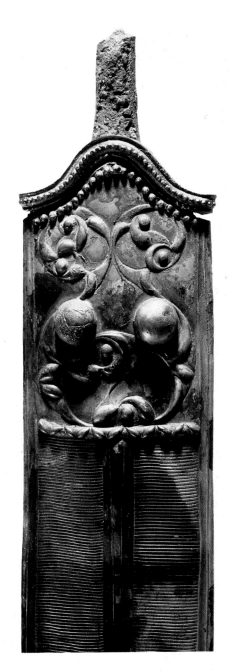

66 Upper part of a bronze scabbard from Little Wittenham, with repouseé ornament (Style V). Width 63mm.

65 Style IV decoration on a bronze scabbard-plate from the River Bann. Width 34mm.

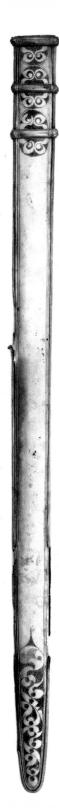

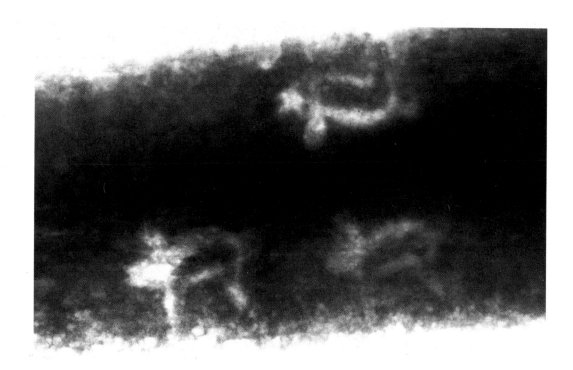

branch of the trade. Whilst some seem to have been forged from a single piece of iron, others have been constructed from several different strips and some very hard blades were achieved. Four other British swords have armourers' marks, including one, found in the River Lark at West Row 68 (Suffolk), only 2km from Isleham, which was stamped twice on one side and once on the other. The West Row blade is in excellent condition: 'its suppleness is extraordinary, and it could be bent back upon itself without breaking' wrote T. C. Lethbridge in 1932 (did he try?). Lethbridge, who frequently brought dry archaeology to life, went on to speculate about the loss of the hilt: 'no doubt the whole weapon flew out of the owner's hand as he was striking a blow and the unfortunate warrior was left gripping the hilt only. It is to be presumed that he did not long survive this

mischance'. More mundane archaeologists would argue that the hilt is likely to have perished after the sword had been discarded, because very few survive – even when the sword is still in its scabbard. Hilts were usually made of wood, often in three parts separated by iron washers and slotted over the tang. An exception is the sword found at Thorpe Hall (N. Humberside) which has a bone hilt ornamented 69 with panels of coloured glass in circular bronze frames.

British warriors seem to have worn little in the way of body armour. Tacitus comments that in their encounters with the Roman army they 'lacked the protection of breast-plates and helmets', but three sites have produced chain-mail dating from the end of La Tène III. It is conceivable that most British fighting men wore nothing at all, for some of their Gallic counterparts are

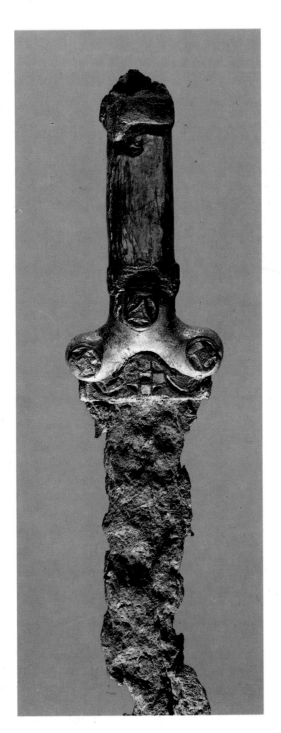

said to have gone naked into battle, and
there are ethnographical parallels for warriors stripping to avoid being encumbered
by clothes. Some British coin-types show a
naked warrior – although this may represent a god or mythical ancestor. There is
some evidence that Celtic warriors protected the head – but again it comes more
from representations and the writings of
classical authors than from archaeological
remains. Several British coins seem to
show warriors with leather helmets, and
Diodorus Siculus records that the Gauls
wore 'bronze helmets which possess large
projecting figures lending the appearance
of enormous stature to the wearer; in some
cases horns form one piece with the
helmet'. The bronze heads which serve as
handle-mounts on the Aylesford bucket
wear large crested helmets, and their
opposite numbers on the Baldock buckets 70
have what seem to be leather helmets with
flabby drooping horns. Horned helmets are
shown on the Gundestrup cauldron from
Denmark, and on stone reliefs from France,
but this tradition is represented by only
one surviving helmet in the whole of
Europe and that like so much fine La Tène
metalwork was dredged from the River
Thames. Found near Waterloo Bridge at 71
some time before 1866, this unique object
with short conical horns was once regarded as a jester's cap. It is covered with a
meandering asymmetrical design whose
relief-work reminded Fox of the Wandsworth round boss and which also has an
affinity with the decoration on the Torrs
chamfrein, but the small repoussé lobes
and shapes with hatched background are
more reminiscent of the style of the Snettisham torque. It seems likely that the
Thames helmet dates from the first century
BC.

The only other surviving Celtic helmet

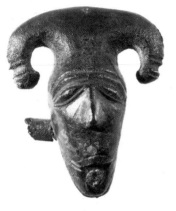

70 *Below* Cast bronze head, a handle-mount from a bucket found at Baldock. Height 51mm.

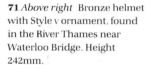

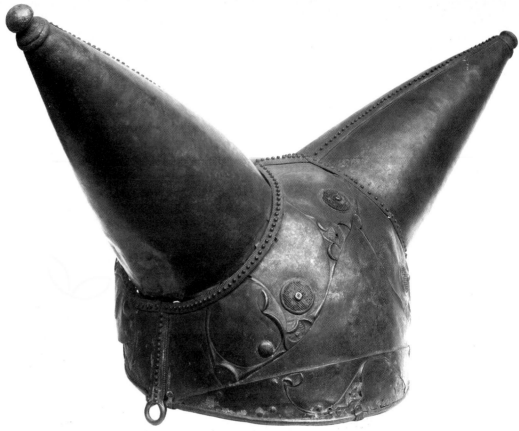

71 *Above right* Bronze helmet with Style v ornament, found in the River Thames near Waterloo Bridge. Height 242mm.

72 *Far right* Bronze helmet, provenance unknown. Height 165mm.

from Britain is of unknown provenance and was formerly in the Meyrick Collection. It too is made of bronze, but is very different in shape and decoration. Its form, a 'jockey-cap', has a long history on the Continent and the British example, whose long 'peak' (which would have been worn at the back, to protect the neck) bears a symmetrical repoussé design, probably dates from shortly after the Roman conquest.

In the absence of body armour, the Celtic warrior defended himself with a shield, for which Britain has produced an impressive body of evidence. The only Celtic shields completely faced with bronze were found in British rivers, and they are important not only for showing the overall shape but also for preserving the entire scheme of decoration. Most Celtic shields were made of wood or leather and by good fortune several have been found on the Continent in waterlogged deposits.

The board of the typical La Tène shield is oval in shape, with a central circular or oval hole covered on the front by a wooden spindle-shaped boss. On the back the hole is crossed horizontally by a strip of wood or iron which forms the handle, so the hand was accommodated in the central hole and protected by the boss. The Battersea shield is the only one in Britain with a metal handle — or rather, a metal handle-cover. A finely decorated thin piece of cut-out bronze borders and crosses the central hand-hole: it leaves space for only a

73

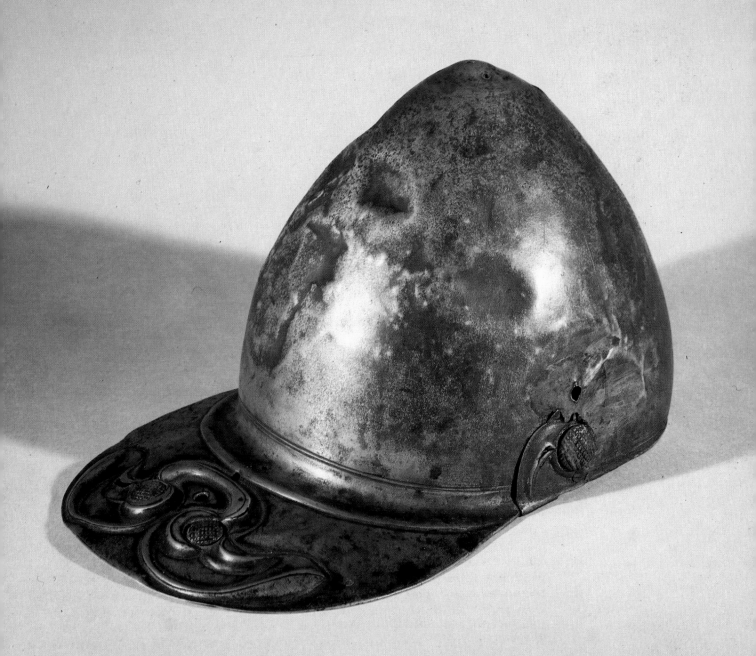

73 Bronze handle-cover from the Battersea shield (see 77). Height 145mm.

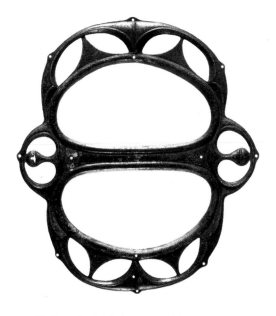

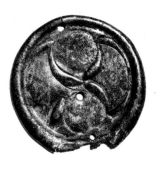

74 Bronze roundel, possibly a shield ornament, with repouseé Style v ornament, from Grimthorpe (see also 42). Diameter 48mm.

small hand, and is too delicate to have taken rough usage – one of the factors suggesting that the Battersea shield was purely ceremonial and not used in battle.

The metal fittings from a grave at Grimthorpe (N. Humberside) give some idea of the appearance of the front of a British shield. A bronze cap surmounted the oval boss and separate lengths of bronze covered the elongated spine of the shield. Two large crescentic bronze plaques were attached to the sides, their inner edges providing the outline of the boss. Shields 'were decorated in individual fashion', according to Diodorus Siculus: they could have been painted or carved, but it is evident that several were fitted with distinctive metal ornaments and this seems the most likely explanation for a small bronze roundel found in the Grimthorpe grave. The step ornament on the Grimthorpe crescentic plaques and the cruciform decoration of the central cap defy close dating, but the small roundel bears a simple design of repoussé lobes which

invites comparison with the Llyn Cerrig Bach plaque and dates from La Tène III. Despite its late date the Grimthorpe shield recalls La Tène I shields on the Continent and may well represent the type then in use in Britain.

Several British shields had the whole of the spindle-shaped boss covered in bronze, with a narrow rim or projections attached to the board, and one with the entire surface of the shield faced with bronze was found in the River Witham in 1826. The covering of its boss and spine together with the two terminal roundels are shaped from a single piece and the rest of the face of the shield is constructed from two bronze sheets. The boss itself, which is slightly above the centre-line of the shield, is exceptionally wide. Its repoussé design springs from the spine, is symmetrical across a diagonal line and seems to be based on a palmette motif. At the centre is a roundel holding three elongated beads of deep-coloured coral with two similar but circular beads in the design at either side. Each terminal roundel had a central petalled boss (only one survives) ringed by an engraved Style IV scroll featuring the half-palmette, and supported by what looks like the head of a fantastic animal with large close-set eyes, petalled ears, and an engraved palmette on a snout which balances on the end of the shield's spine. This magnificent shield has been still further decorated across its full width with what seems to have been a boar with incredibly spindly legs. Only the outline of the creature can be distinguished, and the rivet-holes once used to attach it.

A very similar shield is represented by a bronze boss found in the Thames at Wandsworth: it too may have been entirely faced with bronze, but only the boss survives. Much shorter than the corresponding

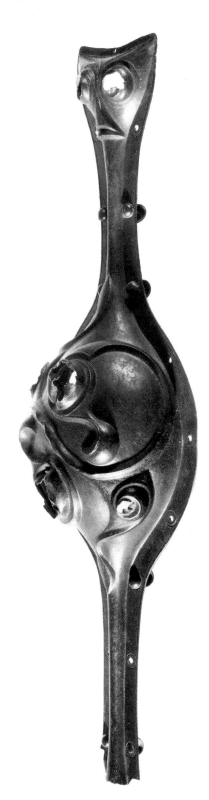

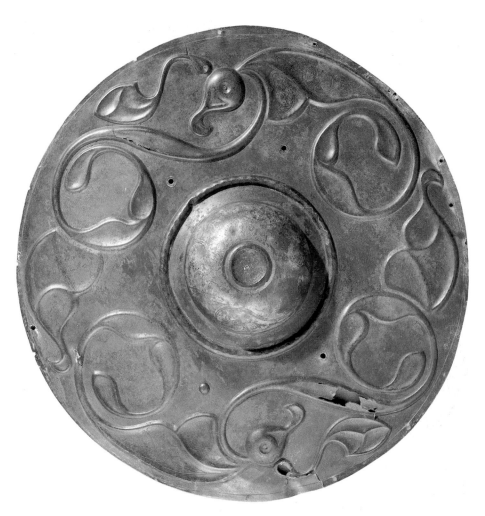

75 *Left* The bronze mask boss from the River Thames at Wandsworth (broken at the bottom end). Length 370mm.

76 *Above* Bronze round boss from the River Thames at Wandsworth. Diameter 330mm.

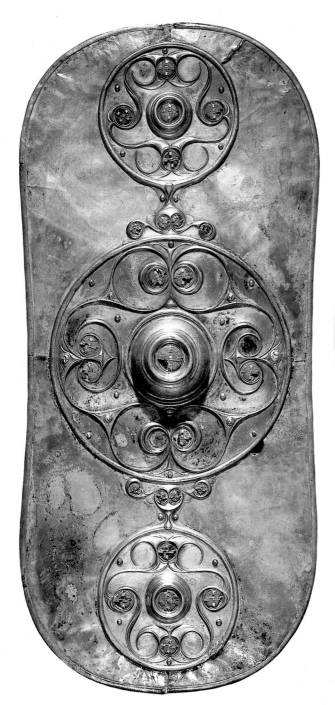

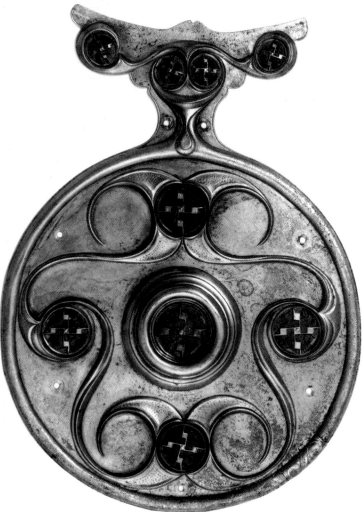

77 *Left* The Battersea shield and, **78** *above*, one of the decorative panels. For other details see front cover and 12. Length 777mm; height of 78 224mm.

piece on the Witham shield it differs in having had separate terminal roundels. The one surviving end of the spine-cover expands to a mask from which it takes its name, the Wandsworth mask boss, and this would have supported the roundel as on the Witham shield. The arrangement of decoration, too, resembles that on the Witham shield, in that it springs from the spine and is diagonally balanced, but the repoussé here is in higher relief and recalls some of the cast 'Plastic Style' works on the Continent. There is only a little engraving, featuring typical Style IV tightly coiled spirals.

Other shields had the spindle-shaped boss covered with iron or bronze in a similar way, and this seems to have been a standard type in the second and first centuries BC. It may be that another form of shield is represented by a circular bronze boss also found in the Thames at Wandsworth. The Wandsworth round boss has 76 distinctive Style IV engraving which resembles that on the Witham shield, although much of it is in the form of disjointed fragments occupying voids within a repoussé design. It has a central dished hemisphere whose broad decorated flange is roughly finished at the edge and was obviously intended to be covered by another sheet (or sheets) of bronze. The shape of this shield is unknown: it could have been circular, but a circular boss does not necessarily imply a circular shield, and the closest parallel for the Wandsworth round boss is on a long shield with rounded ends – the most famous of all British Iron Age antiquities, the Battersea shield.

Like the Witham shield, the Battersea shield is in fact the bronze face and 77 binding of a shield which was probably made of wood. Despite their markedly different bosses the two shields are in some way related, for both have circular terminal panels which are linked to the central element by features which remind us of animal heads. On the Witham shield, and the Wandsworth mask boss, these heads face inwards because they are supporting broad roundels and narrowing through the snout to the spine of the shield; but on the Battersea shield the position is reversed – the broader element is at the centre and the animals face outwards. These Battersea animals have 78 wide spreading antlers, and are made in one piece with the terminal roundels but quite separately from the central boss. The three panels, all with highly accomplished, steeply profiled repoussé decoration, form the central part of a shield whose background is filled with four shaped bronze sheets – each one occupying a quadrant – and they are attached by rivets which pass through panel, sheet bronze and then underlying wood. The repoussé design on the central panel is based on an enclosed palmette which gives rise to triangular shapes on either side. Strands from the other two corners of the triangles then meet to form a circle. This motif occupies one half of the panel and is almost mirrored by the design in the other half; almost mirrored, but not quite, because there are slight differences in some of the infillings. The end panels carry similar but not exactly identical designs based on interlocking s-motifs. Prominent on both end and central panels are a series of roundels built from cast bronze frames into which a soft and malleable red glass, or 'enamel', has been pressed from the underside.

6 Chariots and harness

For their journeys and in battle they use two-horse chariots, the chariot carrying both charioteer and chieftain. When they meet with cavalry in the battle they cast their javelins at the enemy and then descending from the chariot join battle with their swords.

DIODORUS SICULUS

The account by Diodorus Siculus refers to Gaul, where the war-chariot became obsolete by the time of the Gallic Wars, but when Caesar invaded Britain he found chariots used in the same way, and more than one century later some tribes in northern Britain were still employing them to resist Agricola. Some idea of the large number of chariots in Britain is given by Caesar's claim that after the British king Cassivellaunus had disbanded most of his troops 'he retained only some four thousand charioteers, with whom he watched our line of march'.

It may be that the Britons used the same vehicle for journeys and for war, but the archaeological evidence is slight and not very helpful. One day a complete chariot may be found in a waterlogged context; as recently as 1968 a complete wooden wheel was found below the water-table at Holme Pierrepont (Notts.), and the excavator did wonder if more of the vehicle was there, but circumstances prevented complete ex-

80 A cart-burial, one of three excavated by J.S. Dent at Wetwang Slack in the summer of 1984 – too late for the finds to be incorporated in the present text. The wheels had been removed from the vehicle and placed flat on the floor of the grave; the skeleton rested on top of the wheels and was accompanied by an iron sword in a bronze and iron scabbard and no fewer than seven spearheads which were scattered across the body. Within the wheel on the right are two iron horse-bits, and on the left a line of five bronze and iron terrets marks the position of the yoke. The wood of the wheel on the left had disintegrated and left cavities in the soil. The excavators pumped polyurethane foam into the cavities to preserve the shape of the felloe and spokes.

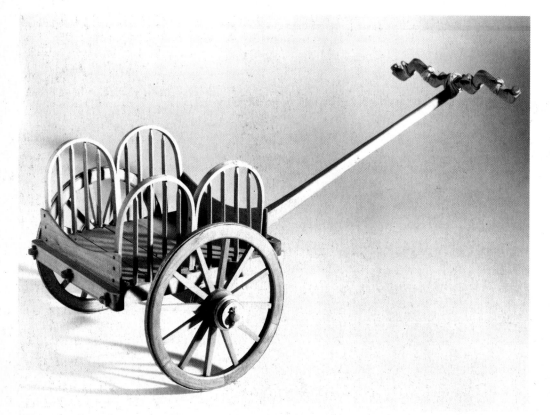

79 A model, giving a suggested reconstruction of a Celtic chariot.

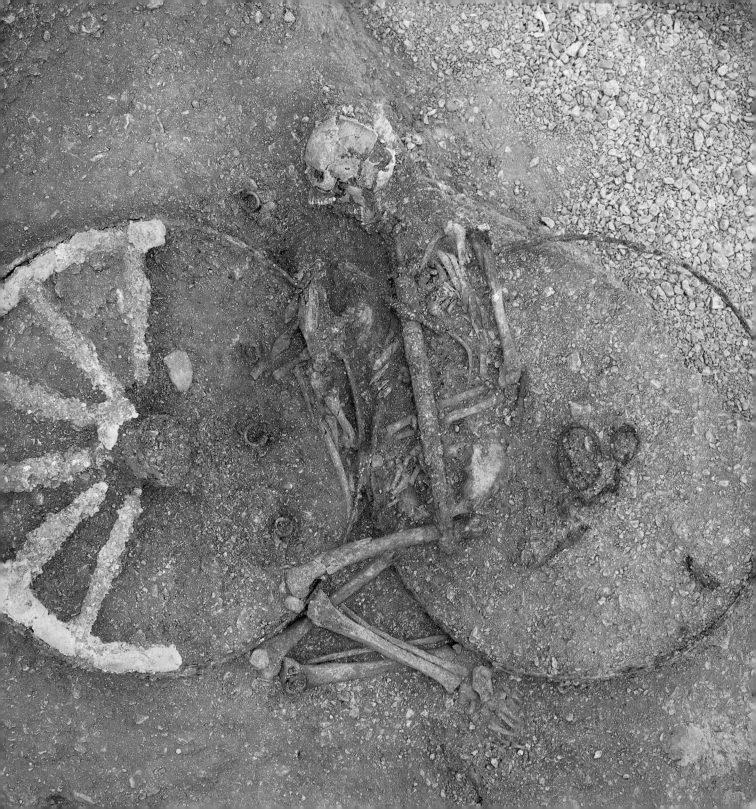

cavation. For the moment models and drawings must be constructed from scant details. [79]

Vehicles were occasionally buried in [80] graves in eastern Yorkshire, but soil conditions preclude the preservation of wood, so only the metal fittings have been found. Most of the Yorkshire vehicles were dismantled, but two near Pickering had been buried complete: both were found with wheels upright and the clear line of a central pole could be traced in the sand of one of the barrows. In a grave at Garton Slack impressions of heavy timbers perhaps represented the axle with the central pole attached, but nothing of the platform or superstructure was found either there or at any other site.

The vehicle in the Yorkshire graves, with two wheels and a central pole, would have been drawn by a pair of horses. In the so-called King's Barrow at Arras both horses had been buried with the vehicle: one was a surprisingly old animal, of no more use in this life, and its burial is consistent with the discovery of a defective horse-bit in the same grave. Only two of the human skeletons in those graves were equipped with personal objects (one had a brooch and another a mirror) and certainly none had weapons, so there is no reason to suppose that the vehicle was intended as a war-chariot. It is best regarded as an all-purpose cart, which perhaps also served as a hearse, and it may have been placed in the grave to indicate the status of the deceased or perhaps to speed his journey to the other world. There was no point in wasting serviceable material on this symbolic journey, hence the worn-out nag and useless horse-bit in the King's Barrow.

The Holme Pierrepont wheel is in excellent condition, and may well have been similar to those in the Yorkshire graves. When found it was associated with a dug-out canoe whose wood has been dated to the Iron Age by Carbon 14. The felloe of the wheel (its wooden circumference) is composed of six segments dowelled together, and each segment takes two spokes: this method of construction, which has remained unchanged to the present day, requires an iron tyre to be heated and then shrunk onto the wheel to clamp all the components tightly together. The wheel has an ash felloe with oak dowells, oak spokes and a birch nave (or hub): a modern wheelwright would choose the same woods for felloe and spokes but he would use elm for the nave.

The wheel was secured to the axle by a linch-pin which may sometimes have been made of hardwood and on one occasion at least was made of antler, but the best-known examples are of metal. The simplest form has bent shank and ring-head forged from a single piece of iron, but there are two other types whose straight iron shanks have bronze terminals. The one has a [83] moulded head, flat on top or capped by a ring: sometimes both the top of the head and the end of the foot are decorated, either in relief or with enamel, and several examples are markedly worn because they have rubbed against the nave. The second type of iron and bronze linch-pin has a crescent-shaped head which provided an ideal field for enamel ornament.

Horse-bits made of iron, bronze or a combination of the two are found in pairs in the Yorkshire graves and in hoards. There are two main designs, one with two [82] links between the rings and the other with three; a prototype of the three-link bit [81] comes from a French burial dated c. 400 BC but in Britain the type was still in use in the first century BC. The two horses would have

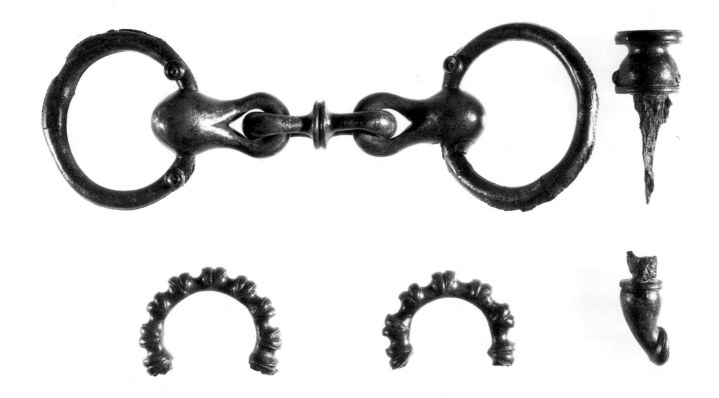

81 Bronze and iron harness from the King's Barrow, Arras: a three-link horse-bit with cast bronze links and rings of iron encased in bronze; a linch-pin whose iron shank has corroded and broken, but the cast-on bronze terminals survive in good condition; and two terrets – the cast-on bronze is well preserved, but the iron bars have corroded and almost disappeared. The horse-bit is 272mm long.

been harnessed one at each side of the central pole, linked by a wooden yoke (the padded horse-collar was a much later development). It seems likely that four terrets (rein-rings) were strapped to the yoke, spaced equidistantly so that the reins of each horse passed through two rings. British Iron Age terrets were D-shaped, cast in bronze or with a straight iron bar onto which a decorative arc of bronze had been cast. But they occur in sets of five, not four, and the fifth terret is always larger than the others and has a broad 'saddle-shaped' bar; it must have occupied a central position, somewhere on the line of the cart-pole, and it may have helped to secure the strapping attaching the yoke to the pole.

The finds from pit 209 at Gussage All Saints suggest that horse-bits, terrets and linch-pins were all manufactured by the same craftsman at the same time, so they were probably acquired in full sets. One such set is seen in the King's Barrow where an undecorated three-link horse-bit is associated with a knobbed terret and a linch-pin with cast bronze head and foot. Rather more elaborate are the products of the Gussage smithy, because some of the side-links of the bits have lobed ornament in relief, and the heads of linch-pins were similarly decorated. The Gussage smith made no fewer than fourteen quite different types of terret. The Polden Hill (Somerset) hoard, dating from the middle of the

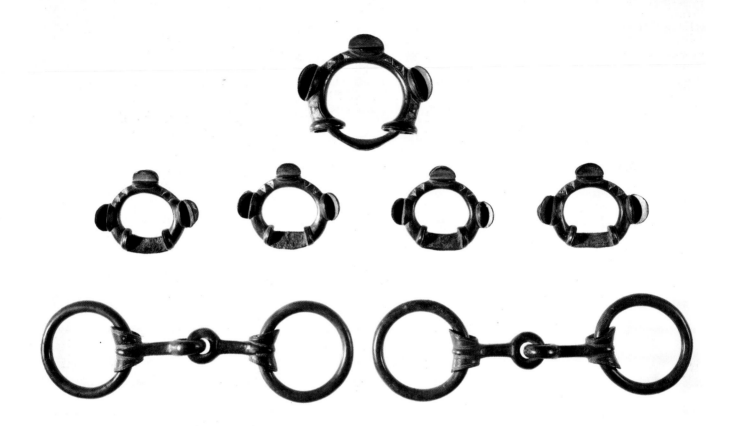

82 A set of bronze harness from Polden Hill: five terrets and two two-link horse-bits. The horse-bits are 220 and 223mm long.

first century AD has matching two-link horse-bits and terrets, but no linch-pins, whereas the Stanwick (N. Yorks.) hoard has sets of three-link bits, terrets and linch-pins. Some of the Stanwick linch-pins were surmounted by shaped rings which closely 83 resemble the terrets. A third type, contemporary with Polden Hill and Stanwick, is represented at Westow (Suffolk) where 83 several enamelled terrets were found. The deep decorative arc of the terret provided an ideal field for champlevé enamel, and there are matching linch-pins with enamelled heads though not found in the same hoard. Horse-bits are occasionally

enamelled, but the fields available for orna- 84 ment are much smaller than those on terrets and linch-pins. Although buckles do not seem to have been used, harness straps must have been fastened and linked in a variety of ways and there is a wide range of strap-links and ornamental fittings, espe- 85 cially from contexts in the first century AD.

One unique piece of horse equipment remains to be discussed. Found in a peat bog, possibly once a loch, at Torrs (Dumfries and Galloway), this remarkable antiquity once belonged to Sir Walter Scott and is now one of the treasures in the National Museum of Antiquities at Edinburgh. It

83 Linch-pins from Kings Langley (*above*) and Stanwick (*below*); and terrets from Westow (*above*) and Stanwick (*below*). The linch-pin and terret at the top have been decorated with champlevé enamel. The Kings Langley linch-pin is 132mm long.

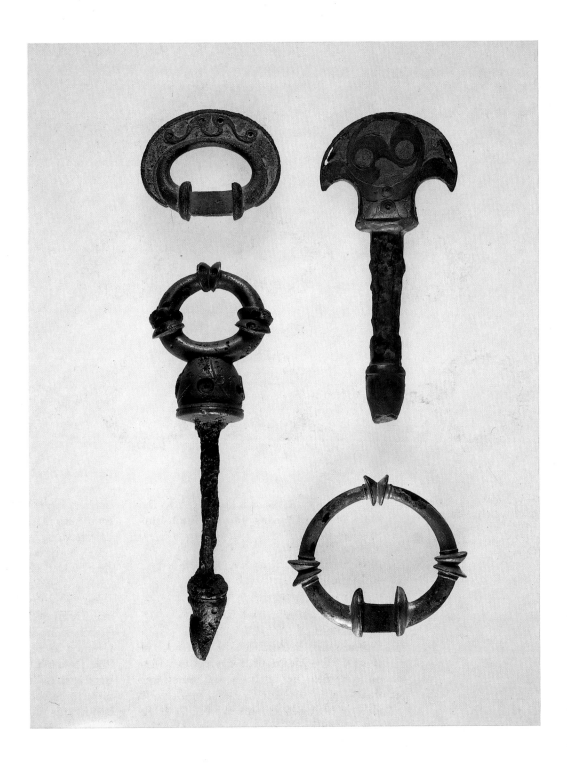

84 Bronze horse-bit, with 'enamel' ornament, from Rise (N. Humberside). This variety was derived from the three-link horse-bit (cf. 81), but here the side-links are cast in one piece with the rein-rings.

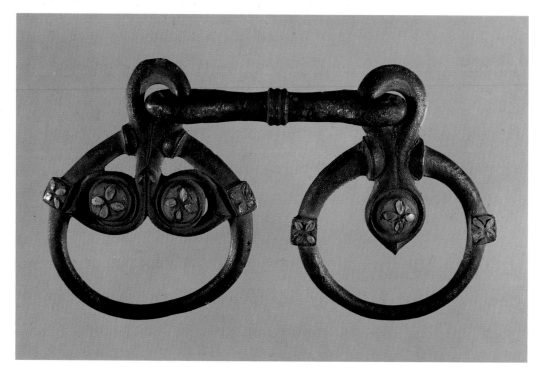

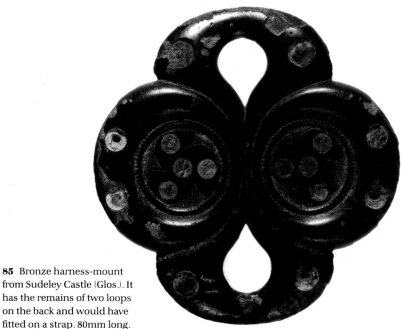

85 Bronze harness-mount from Sudeley Castle (Glos.). It has the remains of two loops on the back and would have fitted on a strap. 80mm long.

used to be regarded as a chamfrein – the **86** piece of armour that covered the frontal of a horse – but detailed study by Piggott and Atkinson showed that it was more complex than had been supposed. It seems that the horns, though approximately contemporary with the head-piece, were attached to it in relatively recent times, but before 1829 when it was first illustrated. The head-piece itself is made from two sheets of bronze decorated with fine, more or less symmetrical repoussé which respects two perforations at the sides and perhaps the damaged remains of another in the centre. There are three engraved repair patches, each disguising a crack in the sheet bronze. Experiments have shown that the head-piece is too small to have been a chamfrein, but it could have been used as a pony-cap: thus the two perforations would be for the ears and not for the eyes, and the conjectural central hole could have taken a plume. The two horns are a pair, though only one retains its cast bird-head terminal. They are decorated with different engraved designs, the motifs and fillings of which may be compared with those on the Witham scabbard (24), Wandsworth round boss (76) and some of the Irish scabbards (64,65). The original function of the horns is obscure: they could have belonged to a horned helmet or have been the terminals of a yoke, but a more attractive notion is that they were mounts for a pair of drinking horns.

Models of British chariots are often shown with a pair of cast bronze hand-holds at the back – the type represented by the 'horn-cap' from Brentford – but the *inside front cover* identification of these objects is only guess-work because none has been found in a context exclusively linked with harness or vehicle fittings. They must have been fitted to a wooden stem and the simplest explanation is that they were mace-heads. It may be that some carts had metal plaques to decorate the woodwork and it is tempting to see some of the Stanwick bronzes in this light. The doleful-looking horse-head – *back cover* the face is created from abstract trumpet-motifs – seems an ideal candidate for a chariot ornament, perhaps bordered by a pair of face-masks in similar style.

The form of the wooden bodywork of the Celtic cart or chariot is obscure, and it may be that different types were used for various specialised purposes. Reconstructions usually show them with an open front, partly because Caesar refers to the British charioteer running up and down the pole and partly because skeletons in some French graves are fully outstretched on the chassis, which would be impossible if the vehicle had a front. But the athletic charioteers would have had no difficulty in springing over a low frame, and the much earlier French vehicles could well have been adapted in order to carry the corpse to the grave. Gallic coins show chariots with a pair of arced frames side by side and a similar vehicle is represented on a stone carving in north Italy. One British coin-type shows a chariot but only two specimens of the coin are known and neither is in good condition.

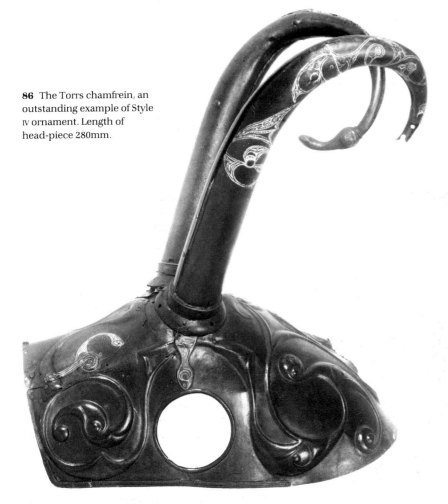

86 The Torrs chamfrein, an outstanding example of Style IV ornament. Length of head-piece 280mm.

7 Ritual

*A grove there was, un-
touched by men's hands
from ancient times, whose
interlacing boughs en-
closed a space of darkness
and cold shade, and
banished the sunlight from
above... gods were worshipped there with savage rites,
the altars were heaped with
hideous offerings, and every tree was sprinkled with
human gore.... The images
of the gods, grim and rude,
were uncouth blocks,
formed of felled tree-
trunks.... The people never
resorted thither to worship
at close quarters, but left
the place to the gods.*

LUCAN – a Roman poet, writing
about a sacred grove destroyed by
Caesar in Gaul

Ritual is of the greatest importance to the study of Celtic art: most of the objects illustrated in this book were probably deposited in accordance with some ritual and the designs which here are coldly classified and ordered could have been full of symbolic meaning to the original behol-ders. The Romans tried to understand Celtic religion in their own terms: 'of the gods they most of all worship Mercury', noted Caesar. He also distinguished two 'classes of men of some dignity and import-ance' – the knights and the druids. 'The druids are concerned with the worship of the gods, look after public and private sacrifice, and expound religious matters'. Druids were also philosophers and teachers, but their activities were deliber-ately shrouded in secrecy and their teachings and traditions were transmitted orally and never committed to writing.

In Britain places of worship certainly included sacred woods, like that described by Lucan in Gaul. Tacitus tells how a Roman governor, Paulinus, desecrated druidic sites in Anglesey (Mona): 'the groves devoted to Mona's barbarous super-stitions he demolished. For it was their religion to drench their altars in the blood of prisoners and consult their gods by means of human entrails'. At the same time in the eastern part of Britain Boudicca's troops were celebrating their rebellion with 'sacrifices, banquets and wanton be-haviour, not only in all their other sacred places, but particularly in the grove of Andate' (Dio Cassius). It seems that the Britons worshipped in temples as well as in groves: one at Hayling Island (Hants.) was a wooden building superseded by a Roman temple built of stone, and it may be that other Roman temples had Iron Age antecedents.

Crudely carved wooden gods reminis-

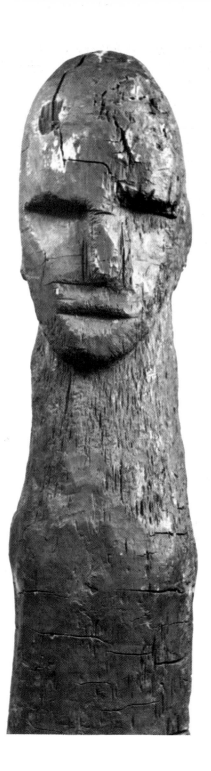

87 Head of a carved wooden figure from Ralaghan (Co. Cavan). The height of the entire figure is 1.14m.

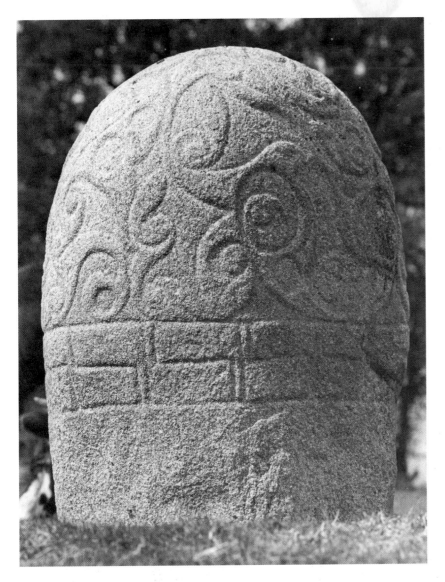

88 The Turoe stone. Height above ground level *c.* 1.2m.

'Celtic' stone heads are known from Bri- 87 tain, but not one has a La Tène context and all must be regarded critically; certainly one of the more convincing examples has recently been identified as Romanesque! Massive carved stones provide surer ground, definitely Celtic and surely ritual. There are five, all in Ireland, of which the most famous is the Turoe stone, a granite 88 erratic covered with carvings which are best related to Style V ornament in England.

Posidonius, quoted by Strabo, tells of treasure found by the Romans at Toulouse: 'part of it being laid up in the temple-enclosures and part in the sacred lakes... the lakes in particular provided inviolability for their treasures'. The type-site at La Tène was interpreted by de Navarro as 'a place where votive offerings were thrown into the water' and Fox used the same explanation for the metalwork from Llyn Cerrig Bach in Anglesey. To these examples might be added the artefacts recovered from certain rivers – especially the weapons and armour from the Witham and the Thames. But it can never be proved that these weapons were deposited according to some ritual, and it is worth recalling that both the Witham and the Thames have produced later (Medieval) and earlier (Bronze Age) weapons. Rivers are natural boundaries, and river-crossings could also be battle-sites; once a weapon has been dropped in deep water in the course of a battle its owner (even if he was lucky enough to survive) stands little chance of recovering it. On the other hand, swords which are still in their scabbards are not so likely to have been dropped by accident and the concentration of finds in selected river-beds does support a ritual explanation. It has been suggested that weapons were dropped into rivers in connection with a burial rite – perhaps in the way that

cent of Lucan's description have been found at the sites of springs in Gaul, and this tradition may be represented by a wooden figure from an Irish bog in County Cavan. A somewhat comparable piece was found in the marshes north of the Thames at Dagenham. But it is very difficult to date such isolated finds. Hundreds of crude

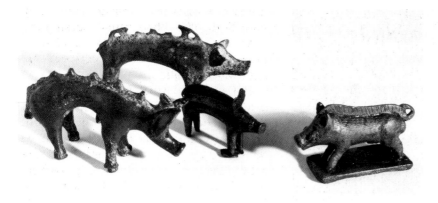

89 Bronze boar figurines: the three on the left are from Hounslow and the other (height 32mm) is from Camerton.

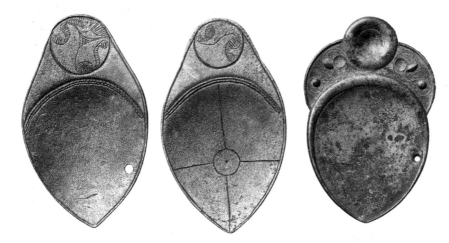

90 A pair of bronze spoons from Crosby Ravensworth and another (length 114mm) from London.

Malory's King Arthur, on the point of death, instructed Sir Bedivere: 'take thou Excalibur, my good sword, and go with it to yonder water side, and when thou comest there I charge thee throw my sword in that water'. This idea is attractive in the absence of a known burial rite in much of southern England before the first century BC when cremation was introduced, but rivers have produced several swords which are contemporary with the cremation rite, and why are mirrors never found in rivers?

Ritual, too, might explain some of the figurines and a few other mysterious bronzes of the British Iron Age. A group of three bronze boar figures was discovered 89 by labourers at Hounslow in 1864 along with two other figurines, possibly dogs, and a model wheel. Two of the boars have high pierced crests (now broken) and the third has the remains of a stand. Perhaps they were all originally on stands, like a more Roman-looking example found recently at Camerton, which resembles a toy from a child's farmyard. Model wheels are known from votive contexts, and a boar is carved on the side of a famous representation of a Gallic god, so this small collection from Hounslow is best interpreted as ritual.

Curious spoons with short decorated handles are also likely to have had a ritual function: often found in pairs, one of which is pierced and the other marked with a cross, they are hardly likely to have been functional. Could they have been used for feeding the gods? The pair from Crosby 90 Ravensworth (Cumbria) is typical, though with uninspired decoration on the handles. They were found some seven or eight metres apart in boggy ground around a spring, 'well known for its copious supply'. The one from London came from the Thames, but others have been found in dry earth and some were with burials. As for

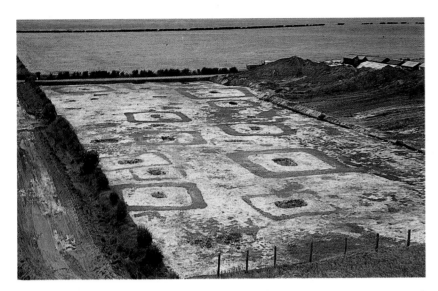

91 *Above* A La Tène cemetery in the course of excavation at Burton Fleming. Centuries of cultivation have completely flattened the barrows, but below the ploughsoil remain the filled-in barrow ditches, distinctively square in plan, and the central graves.

92 *Below* Bronze disc from Ireland. Diameter 280mm.

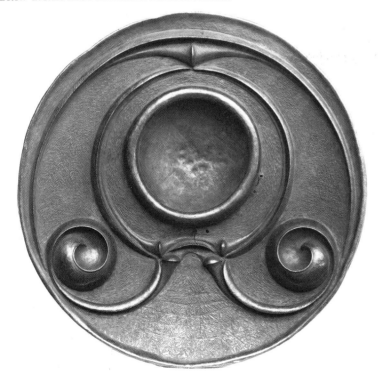

the bronze discs from Ireland, could they 92 have been other than ritual? Seven such discs are known, each with a circular hollow, slightly off-centre, bordered by high relief scrolls.

The ultimate ritual was burial of the dead. According to Diodorus Siculus the Gauls believed 'that the souls of men are immortal, and that after a definite number of years they live a second life when the soul passes into another body'. Beliefs must have varied considerably across the Celtic world, and in Britain several different burial practices were observed. In Yorkshire the corpses were buried and then covered by small barrows raised by cutting square-plan ditches around the grave. 91 Such barrows were grouped in cemeteries but most of them have been flattened by centuries of ploughing and only recently identified by aerial photography. The Yorkshire skeletons are crouched or contracted, and some were accompanied by simple grave-goods, such as a brooch or a joint of meat. In the rest of Britain burials are rare until the first century BC, when cremation was introduced: before that the few graves known are obviously those of a minority of the population and the normal rite has left no trace whatsoever. Most often cremations comprise only an urn to house the burnt bones, but some are more elaborate and have accessory vessels and metal grave-goods. The richest burials, in terms of the number of artefacts deposited, are centred in Hertfordshire and have large graves fully equipped with objects connected with eating and drinking. Some went to the grave with fire-dogs for the hearth and a cauldron for preparing food, and most faced the life hereafter with Dutch courage – a grave found at Welwyn 52 Garden City in 1965 had five amphorae which together would have held about

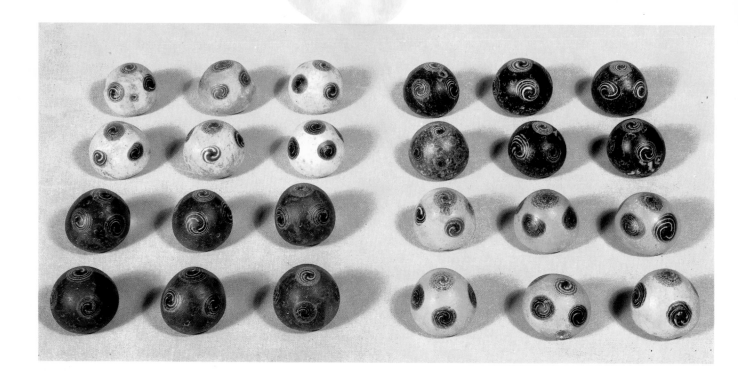

93 Glass game-pieces from a grave at Welwyn Garden City. Height 20 – 22mm.

twenty-five gallons of Italian wine. That burial also had an Italian silver cup and no fewer than thirty pots arranged on the floor of the grave. The most spectacular item, however, was a set of unique glass game pieces: divided by colour into four sets of six pieces, they were intended for a race-game such as ludo. Grave-goods may have been deposited to indicate the status of the dead, or to provide them for a journey or with equipment needed in the afterlife. Archaeologists are left to speculate about the beliefs which have provided such an important source of artefacts.

The Celtic art that remains for study today forms an odd selection, and not a fair sample of what was made and used by the Britons. Much of it was recovered in unenlightening circumstances, because less than 20 per cent came from archaeological excavations – and that includes nineteenth-century excavations. More than 70 per cent of the objects illustrated in this book were deliberately buried: about 30 per cent were in graves, and a similar percentage in rivers or other watery deposits, whilst some 10 per cent came from hoards. Of the rest, many are isolated finds whose precise context is unknown. Metalwork is represented disproportionately because of its high rate of survival: wood, leather and even skin was probably decorated but hardly any of these materials has been preserved. However, in spite of its limitations, this selection is more than enough to show that the British contribution to Celtic art was second to none, and to establish Celtic art as one of the outstanding abstract arts in world history.

Bibliography

Through the kindness of Professor Jope I have read the proofs of the standard work *Early Celtic Art in the British Isles* (by P. Jacobsthal and E. M. Jope) soon to be published by Oxford University Press; hitherto the most recent survey devoted to the British material alone was *Pattern and Purpose* by Sir Cyril Fox (1958). For the Continent P. Jacobsthal's *Early Celtic Art* (1944, reprinted 1969) is still fundamental, whilst more recent volumes dealing with both British and continental Celtic art are P.-M. Duval's *Les Celtes* (1977) and J. V. S. Megaw's *Art of the European Iron Age* (1970) – Megaw is currently preparing a revised version. A full survey of artefacts in Scotland and northern England is given by Morna MacGregor, *Early Celtic Art in North Britain* (1976): the Yorkshire burials are dealt with by I. M. Stead's *The Arras Culture* (1979); and there is now an excellent catalogue of the Irish material by Barry Raftery, *A Catalogue of Irish Iron Age Antiquities* (1983). Useful text-books of the British Iron Age, with full bibliographies, have been written by B. W. Cunliffe (*Iron Age Communities in Britain*, second edition, 1978) and D. W. Harding (*The Iron Age in Lowland Britain*, 1974).

Coins rank amongst the finest examples of Celtic art, and provide a wealth of information about the Britons, but they have been excluded from the present book because they bear little relationship to other art forms: for an excellent introduction see Derek Allen's *An Introduction to Celtic Coins* (1978).

Books, however, are no substitute for looking at the objects themselves. The British Museum has an incomparable collection, and very good examples exist elsewhere.

Acknowledgements

All the objects illustrated in this book are in the British Museum, except those listed below. The author and publishers are grateful to the copyright holders for permission to reproduce the photographs.

Ashmolean Museum, Oxford 66
Bedford Museum 54
Cambridge University Museum of Archaeology 39, 68
Hull Museum 59 (photo A.L. Pacitto)
Letchworth Museum 11, 70
Luton Museum 55
Museum of Antiquities of the University and Society of Antiquaries of Newcastle upon Tyne 36
Museum of London *inside front cover*
National Museum, Dublin 44, 87
National Museum of Antiquities of Scotland 86
National Museum of Wales 17, 28
Collection of the Duke of Northumberland, Alnwick Castle 24
Reading Museum 63
Salisbury Museum 23 (right)
Somerset County Museum, Taunton 51 (photo A.L. Pacitto)
State Hermitage Museum, Leningrad 31
Wisbech and Fenland Museum 18
Yorkshire Museum, York 21, 34, 37, 41, 69, 81

Plate 1 is by Aerofilms Ltd; 7 R.L. Wilkins; 52 and 91 I.M. Stead; 80 A.L. Pacitto; 88 Commissioners of Public Works in Ireland; and 14 is from a photograph in the possession of E.M. Jope.

Many of the photographs were taken in the British Museum by Victor Bowley; line drawings were prepared by Philip Compton, Meredydd Moores and Robert Pengelly; and the text and arrangement of the book has been much improved by Jenny Chattington.

Index